Reach the Highes
Professional Learni..g. Leadership

VOLUMES IN THE REACH THE HIGHEST STANDARD IN PROFESSIONAL LEARNING SERIES

Learning Communities

Leadership

Resources

Data

Learning Designs

Implementation

Outcomes

Reach the Highest Standard in Professional Learning: Leadership

Karen Seashore Louis
Shirley M. Hord
Valerie von Frank

A Joint Publication

CORWIN
A SAGE Company

learningforward

FOR INFORMATION:

Corwin

A SAGE Company

2455 Teller Road

Thousand Oaks, California 91320

(800) 233-9936

www.corwin.com

SAGE Publications Ltd.

1 Oliver's Yard

55 City Road

London EC1Y 1SP

United Kingdom

SAGE Publications India Pvt. Ltd.

B 1/I 1 Mohan Cooperative Industrial Area

Mathura Road, New Delhi 110 044

India

SAGE Publications Asia-Pacific Pte. Ltd.

3 Church Street

#10-04 Samsung Hub

Singapore 049483

Printed in the United States of America

Library of Congress Cataloging-in-Publication Data

Names: Louis, Karen Seashore, author. | Hord, Shirley M., author. | Von Frank, Valerie, author.

Title: Reach the highest standard in professional learning. Leadership / Karen Seashore Louis, Shirley M. Hord, Valerie von Frank.

Other titles: Leadership.

Description: Thousand Oaks, California : Corwin/Leaning Forward, a SAGE Company, 2016. | Series: Reach the highest standard in professional learning series | Includes bibliographical references and index.

Identifiers: LCCN 2016005112 | ISBN 9781452292137 (pbk. : alk. paper)

Subjects: LCSH: Educational leadership—United States. | Professional learning communities—United States. | Teachers—In-service training—United States.

Classification: LCC LB2805 .L575 2016 | DDC 371.2—dc23 LC record available at https://lccn.loc.gov/2016005112

This book is printed on acid-free paper.

Program Director: Dan Alpert

Senior Associate Editor: Kimberly Greenberg

Editorial Assistant: Katie Crilley

Production Editor: Amy Schroller

Copy Editor: Michelle Ponce

Typesetter: C&M Digitals (P) Ltd.

Proofreader: Ellen Brink

Indexer: Judy Hunt

Cover Designer: Gail Buschman

Marketing Manager: Charline Maher

SFI Certified Sourcing
www.sfiprogram.org
SFI-00453

16 17 18 19 20 10 9 8 7 6 5 4 3 2 1

Contents

Introduction to the Series

These are the demands on educators and school systems right now, among many others:

- They must fulfill the moral imperative of educating every child for tomorrow's world, regardless of background or status.
- They must be prepared to implement college- and career-ready standards and related assessments.
- They must implement educator evaluations tied to accountability systems.

A critical element in creating school systems that can meet these demands is building the capacity of the system's educators at all levels, from the classroom teacher to the instructional coach to the school principal to the central office administrator, and including those partners who work within and beyond districts. Building educator capacity in this context requires effective professional learning.

Learning Forward's Standards for Professional Learning define the essential elements of and conditions for professional learning that leads to changed educator practices and improved student results. They are grounded in the understanding that the ultimate purpose of professional learning is increasing student success. Educator effectiveness—and this includes all educators working in and with school systems, not just teachers—is linked closely to student learning. Therefore increasing the effectiveness of educators is a key lever to school improvement.

Effective professional learning happens in a culture of continuous improvement, informed by data about student and educator performance and supported by leadership and sufficient resources. Educators learning daily have access to information about relevant instructional strategies and resources and, just as important, time for collaboration with colleagues, coaches, and school leaders. Education leaders and systems that value effective professional learning provide not only sufficient time and money but also create structures that reinforce monitoring and evaluation of that learning so they understand what is effective and have information to adjust and improve.

WHY STANDARDS?

Given that any system can—and must—develop expertise about professional learning, why are standards important? Among many reasons are these:

First, adherence to standards ensures equity. When learning leaders across schools and systems agree to follow a common set of guidelines, they are committing to equal opportunities for all the learners in those systems. If all learning is in alignment with the Standards for Professional Learning and tied to student and school improvement goals, then all educators have access to the best expertise available to improve their practice and monitor results.

Standards also provide a common language that allows for conversation, collaboration, and implementation planning that crosses state, regional, and national borders. This collaboration can leverage expertise from any corner of the world to change practice and results.

Finally, standards offer guidelines for accountability. While an endorsement of the standards doesn't in itself guarantee quality, they provide a framework within which systems can establish measures to monitor progress, alignment, and results.

FROM STANDARDS TO TRANSFORMATION

So a commitment to standards is a first critical step. Moving into deep understanding and sustained implementation of standards is another matter. Transforming practices, and indeed, whole systems, will require long-term study, planning, and evaluation.

Reach the Highest Standard in Professional Learning is created to be an essential set of tools to help school and system leaders take those steps. As with the Standards for Professional Learning themselves, there will be seven volumes, one for each standard.

While the standards were created to work in synergy, we know that educators approach professional learning from a wide range of experiences, concerns, expertise, and passions. Perhaps a school leader may have started PLCs in his school to address a particular learning challenge, and thus has an abiding interest in how learning communities can foster teacher quality and better results. Maybe a central office administrator started her journey to standards-based professional learning through a study of how data informs changes, and she wants to learn more about the foundations of data use. This series was created to support such educators and to help them continue on their journey of understanding systemwide improvement and the pieces that make such transformation possible.

In developing this series of books on the Standards for Professional Learning, Corwin and Learning Forward envisioned that practitioners would enter this world of information through one particular book, and that their needs and interests would take them to all seven as the books are developed. The intention is to serve the range of needs practitioners bring and to support a full understanding of the elements critical to effective professional learning.

All seven volumes in Reach the Highest Standard in Professional Learning share a common structure, with components to support knowledge development, exploration of changes in practice, and a vision of each concept at work in real-world settings.

In each volume, readers will find

- A think piece developed by a leading voice in the professional learning field. These thought leaders represent both scholars and practitioners, and their work invites readers to consider the foundations of each standard and to push understanding of those seven standards.
- An implementation piece that helps readers put the think piece and related ideas into practice, with tools for both individuals and groups to use in reflection and discussion about the standards. Shirley M. Hord and Patricia Roy, long-standing Learning Forward standards leaders, created the implementation pieces across the entire series.

- A case study that illuminates what it looks like in schools and districts when education leaders prioritize the standards in their improvement priorities. Valerie von Frank, with many years of writing about education in general and professional learning in particular, reported these pieces, highlighting insights specific to each standard.

MOVING TOWARD TRANSFORMATION

We know this about effective professional learning: Building awareness isn't enough to change practice. It's a critical first piece, and these volumes will help in knowledge development. But sustaining knowledge and implementing change require more.

Our intention is that the content and structure of the volumes can move readers from awareness to changes in practice to transformation of systems. And of course transformation requires much more. Commitment to a vision for change is an exciting place to start. A long-term informed investment of time, energy, and resources is non-negotiable, as is leadership that transcends one visionary leader who will inevitably move on.

Ultimately, it will be the development of a culture of collective responsibility for all students that sustains improvement. We invite you to begin your journey toward developing that culture through study of the Standards for Professional Learning and through Reach the Highest Standard in Professional Learning. Learning Forward will continue to support the development of knowledge, tools, and evidence that inform practitioners and the field. Next year's challenges may be new ones, and educators working at their full potential will always be at the core of reaching our goals for students.

Stephanie Hirsh
Executive Director, Learning Forward

The Learning Forward Standards for Professional Learning

Learning Communities: Professional learning that increases educator effectiveness and results for all students occurs within learning communities committed to continuous improvement, collective responsibility, and goal alignment.

Leadership: Professional learning that increases educator effectiveness and results for all students requires skillful leaders who develop capacity, advocate, and create support systems for professional learning.

Resources: Professional learning that increases educator effectiveness and results for all students requires prioritizing, monitoring, and coordinating resources for educator learning.

Data: Professional learning that increases educator effectiveness and results for all students uses a variety of sources and types of student, educator, and system data to plan, assess, and evaluate professional learning.

Learning Designs: Professional learning that increases educator effectiveness and results for all students integrates theories, research, and models of human learning to achieve its intended outcomes.

Implementation: Professional learning that increases educator effectiveness and results for all students applies research on change and sustains support for implementation of professional learning for long-term change.

Outcomes: Professional learning that increases educator effectiveness and results for all students aligns its outcomes with educator performance and student curriculum standards.

Source: Learning Forward. (2015). *Standards for Professional Learning.* Oxford, OH: Author.

The Leadership Standard

Professional learning that increases educator effectiveness and results for all students requires skillful leaders who develop capacity, advocate, and create support systems for professional learning.

Leaders throughout the preK–12 education community recognize effective professional learning as a key strategy for supporting significant school and school system improvements to increase results for all students. Whether they lead from classrooms, schools, school systems, technical assistance agencies, professional associations, universities, or public agencies, leaders develop their own and others' capacity to learn and lead professional learning, advocate for it, provide support systems, and distribute leadership and responsibility for its effectiveness and results.

DEVELOP CAPACITY FOR LEARNING AND LEADING

Leaders hold learning among their top priorities for students, staff, and themselves. Leaders recognize that universal high expectations for all students require ambitious improvements in curriculum, instruction, assessment, leadership practices, and support systems. These improvements require effective professional learning to expand educators' knowledge, skills, practices, and dispositions. All leaders demand effective professional learning focused on substantive results for themselves, their colleagues, and their students. Leaders artfully combine deep understanding of and cultural responsiveness to the community they serve with high expectations and support for results to achieve school and school system goals. They embed professional learning into the organization's vision by communicating that it is a core function for improvement and by establishing and maintaining a public and persistent focus on educator professional learning. Leaders of professional learning are found at the classroom, school, and system levels. They set the agenda for professional learning by aligning it to classroom, school, and school system goals for student and educator learning, using data to monitor and measure its effects on educator student performance. They may facilitate professional learning, coach and supervise those who facilitate it, or do both. As facilitators of professional learning, they apply a body of technical knowledge and skills to plan, design, implement, and evaluate professional learning. As coaches and supervisors of those who facilitate professional learning, they develop expertise in others about effective professional learning, set high standards for their performance, and use data to give frequent, constructive feedback.

To engage in constructive conversations about the alignment of student and educator performance, leaders cultivate a culture based on the norms of high expectations, shared responsibility, mutual respect, and relational trust. They work collaboratively with others, such as school and system based resource personnel and external technical assistance providers, so that all educators engage in effective job-embedded or external professional learning to meet individual, team, school, and system goals.

Systems that recognize and advance shared leadership promote leaders from all levels of the organizations. Leaders can hold formal roles, such as principal, instructional coach, or task force chair, for long periods of time or informal roles, such as voluntary mentor or spokesperson, for shorter periods. All leaders share responsibility for student achievement among members of the school and community. Leaders hold themselves and others accountable for the quality and results of professional learning. Leaders work collaboratively with others to create a vision for academic success and set clear goals for student achievement based on educator and student learning data.

ADVOCATE FOR PROFESSIONAL LEARNING

Leaders clearly articulate the critical link between increased student learning and educator professional learning. As supporters of professional learning, they apply understanding of organizational and human changes to design needed conditions, resources, and other supports for learning and change.

As advocates for professional learning, leaders make their own career-long learning visible to others. They participate in professional learning within and beyond their own work environment. Leaders consume information in multiple fields to enhance their leadership practice. Through learning, they clarify their values and beliefs and their influence on others and on the achievement of organizational goals. Their actions model attitudes and behavior they expect of all educators.

CREATE SUPPORT SYSTEMS AND STRUCTURES

Skillful leaders establish organizational systems and structures that support effective professional learning and ongoing continuous improvement. They equitably distribute resources to accomplish individual, team, school, and school system goals. Leaders actively engage with policy makers and decision makers so that resources, policies, annual calendars, daily schedules, and structures support professional learning to increase student achievement. Leaders create and align policies and guidelines to ensure effective professional learning within their school systems or schools. They work within national, regional, and local agencies to adopt standards, monitor implementation, and evaluate professional learning's effectiveness and results.

Source: Learning Forward. (2015). *Standards for Professional Learning.* Oxford, OH: Author.

About the Authors

**Dr. Karen Seashore Louis** is a Regents professor and the Robert H. Beck Chair in the Department of Organizational Policy, Leadership, and Development at the University of Minnesota. She has also served as the director of the Center for Applied Research and Educational Improvement at the University of Minnesota, department chair, and associate dean of the College of Education and Human Development. Her work focuses on school improvement and reform, school effectiveness, leadership in school settings, and the politics of knowledge use in education. Her most recent books include *Building Strong School Cultures: A Guide to Leading Change* (with Sharon Kruse, 2009), *Linking Leadership to Student Learning* (with Kenneth Leithwood, 2011), *and Educational Policy: Political Culture and Its Effects* (2012).

A fellow of the American Educational Research Association, she also served as the vice president of Division A, on the executive board of the University Council for Educational Administration, and recently as a member of the "field knowledge" study group to provide input to the recently revised national leadership preparation standards. Karen is actively involved with school administrators, both in her research and in professional development. She has advised 70 doctoral candidates over her career, the majority of whom are in educational leadership positions.

She has received numerous awards, including the Lifetime Contributions to Staff Development award from the National Staff Development Association (2007), the Campbell Lifetime Achievement

Award from the University Council for Educational Administration (2009), and a Life Member designation from the International Congress for School Effectiveness and School Improvement.

 **Dr. Shirley M. Hord**, is the scholar laureate of Learning Forward (previously National Staff Development Council), following her retirement as scholar emerita at the Southwest Educational Development Laboratory in Austin, Texas. There she directed the Strategies for Increasing Student Success Program. She continues to design and coordinate professional development activities related to educational change and improvement, school leadership, and the creation of professional learning communities.

Her early roles as elementary school classroom teacher and university science education faculty at the University of Texas at Austin were followed by her appointment as codirector of Research on the Improvement Process at the Research and Development Center for Teacher Education at The University of Texas at Austin. There she administered and conducted research on school improvement and the role of school leaders in school change.

She served as a fellow of the National Center for Effective Schools Research and Development and was U.S. representative to the Foundation for the International School Improvement Project, an international effort that develops research, training, and policy initiatives to support local school improvement practices.

In addition to working with educators at all levels across the United States and Canada, Hord makes presentations and consults in Asia, Europe, Australia, Africa, and Mexico.

Her current interests focus on the creation and functioning of educational organizations as learning communities and the role of leaders who serve such organizations. Hord is the author of numerous articles and books, of which a selection of the most recent are *Implementing Change: Patterns, Principles, and Potholes,* 4th ed. (with Gene E. Hall, 2015); *Reclaiming Our Teaching Profession: The Power of Educators Learning in Community* (with Edward F. Tobia, 2012); and *A Playbook for Professional Learning: Putting the Standards Into Action* (with Stephanie Hirsh, 2012).

Valerie von Frank is an author, editor, and communications consultant. A former newspaper editor and education reporter, she has focused much of her writing on education issues, including professional learning. She served as communications director in an urban school district and a nonprofit school reform organization and was the editor for seven years of *JSD,* the flagship magazine for the National Staff Development Council, now Learning Forward. She has written extensively for education publications, including *JSD, Tools for Schools, The Learning System, The Learning Principal,* and *T3.* She is coauthor with Ann Delehant of *Making Meetings Work: How to Get Started, Get Going, and Get It Done* (Corwin, 2007); with Linda Munger of *Change, Lead, Succeed* (National Staff Development Council, 2010); with Robert Garmston of *Unlocking Group Potential to Improve Schools* (Corwin, 2012); and with Jennifer Abrams of *The Multigenerational Workplace: Communicate, Collaborate, and Create Community* (Corwin, 2014).

CHAPTER ONE

Leadership for Professional Learning

Creating the Learning Organization

Karen Seashore Louis

> Leadership: Professional learning that increases educator effectiveness and results for all students requires skillful leaders who develop capacity, advocate, and create support systems for professional learning. (Learning Forward, 2011)

Neither educators nor policy makers question the role of leadership in creating more effective schools. Even as we acknowledge that classroom teachers are the most important adults in a student's life, we know that the teacher leaders, principals, and district staff members who stand behind them either enhance or diminish their ability to develop. The consequence of good leadership is the classroom magic that engages young people in their initial steps toward becoming successful, adaptive adults.

Recently much attention has been given to the larger question of whether the actions of school leaders can have any impact on the bottom line of student learning. While that question will receive some attention in this chapter, the primary focus is on how leaders and leadership affect the learning of other adults in the school. More particularly, the emphasis will be on the way in which school leaders can create a school culture in which all adults see themselves as part of the larger enterprise of continuous learning. Thus, the focus is on those who have responsibilities that include supporting adult professional learning in schools. This, book will not engage deeply with the nuts and bolts that are the critical emphasis of many of the standards for professional learning (Learning Forward, 2011). Instead, it will focus on understanding the pathways by which leaders orchestrate the learning environment, allowing teachers to take charge of their learning.

The chapter is organized around the main topics that are shown in Figure 1.1, which reworks a framework developed to create challenging college programs (Fink, 2013). The data I present draw on recent research about school leadership, including the work of my colleagues and me on a large national study. The topics include the following:

- *Foundations*: Assumptions underlying the Learning Forward standards and what leaders need to know about how their work affects teacher and student growth
- *Integration*: How the work of leaders helps to keep the school focused on professional development and learning that addresses significant areas of growth for a school
- *The Human Dimension*: What leaders do to foster professional communities that lead to organizational learning
- *Caring*: Why the emotional side of leadership is critical in creating a strong, learning adaptive school
- *Learning How to Learn*: A summary of the elements of a school culture that foster organization learning, with a focus on those that may require leader development

This volume and chapter are grounded in the assumption that all members of a school are responsible for learning and growing, but that administrators and teachers in formal leadership positions have a particular responsibility for creating the culture and structures that make adult learning a vibrant and visible component of their daily work. As is clear in the *Standards for Professional Learning* and related publications, learning communities (also known as professional communities and communities of practice) are the site for *collaborative* teacher learning. While these can often emerge spontaneously, when teachers

Figure 1.1 Leadership for Professional Learning Framework

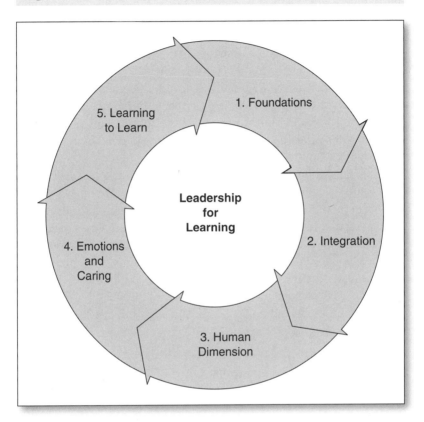

or others who share an interest come together to share ideas, they are most often nurtured in schools and districts where leaders give priority to creating supportive conditions for engagement. What these are, and how they can be deliberately fostered, is what this and the other chapters in this book are about.

FOUNDATIONS

LEADERSHIP IS IMPORTANT—IN NEW WAYS

Leadership and learning are indispensable to each other.

—John F. Kennedy[1]

It is hardly surprising that the leadership standard comes second to the foundational standard of learning communities in the 2011 version of the *Standards for Professional Learning*. We have known for a long time that principals and district administrators have a big impact on teachers' experience of their work life. From Willard Waller's pungent observations about teachers' lives in high schools in the 1930s to Richard Ingersoll's research documenting how principals contribute to high teacher turnover in less effective schools, we see that formal leaders are critical (Ingersoll, Hoxby, & Scrupski, 2004; Waller, 1932). The earliest efforts by the National Staff Development Council (now Learning Forward) to develop standards for professional development emphasized the role of leadership:

> An essential element . . . is skillful leadership on the part of principals and district administrators. These leaders must help create community-wide consensus regarding a compelling vision that embodies high expectations for student learning, teaching, and staff development. In addition, they must be "keepers of the dream" who frequently remind everyone of the school's values and core beliefs. (Killion, 1999, p. xi)

The Leader's Job: New and Complex

Principals have always had responsibility for making sure that their schools are well managed, that student behavior is acceptable to teachers and other stakeholders, and that the "core technology" of teaching is insulated from disruption. According to Richard Rossmiller, this traditional perspective on a school leader's responsibilities was hardly challenged (and was well-ensconced in most principal preparation programs) throughout the high-innovation years of the 1970s and '80s (Rossmiller, 1992). Even today, when so many leadership scholars trumpet the need for transformational leadership, it is clear that a solid and effective approach to managing the school is an essential feature of what good administrators do to make teachers' work easier—and is associated with improvements in student learning (Grissom & Loeb, 2011; Horng & Loeb, 2010).

Still, although the need to manage schools has persisted, the world of school administration has changed a great deal since the early 2000s. Principals are increasingly accountable for the quality of the student learning in the schools that they head, and (for the first time) district administrators have also been informed that they are responsible for the performance of the schools that they oversee. The urgency associated with school improvement has become a political reality in the United States (and other countries) with the initiation of public, comparable measures of student performance, and administrators (even more than teachers) are on the hot seat.

Since principals and district administrators can have direct impacts on only a few students, they have increasingly been urged to improve their schools by improving teaching. As Guskey notes, a rush to do this through formal mass professional development programs was a nonstarter: Too little was known at that time about what constitutes formal learning opportunities that would actually affect classrooms and students. Furthermore, in spite of years of debate and a deluge of research on effective teaching, most scholars concluded that there was more variation in the quality of instruction between classrooms in the same school than between schools (Guskey, 2003). These constraints—weak knowledge about effective programs that would have known impacts on individual teachers *and* concerns about within-school variation in teaching—led to a reaffirmation of some key axioms of older school improvement research: (1) the school is the unit that is most amenable to significant change, and (2) to create that change involves challenging conventional thinking (Hallinger & Murphy, 1986; Heckman, Oakes, & Sirotnik, 1983).

What did this mean for school leadership? To a great extent, it suggested a radical reorientation away from traditional management functions toward "instructional leadership" that encompassed the assumption of responsibility for guiding improvement in every classroom. In practice, the idea was exceptionally poorly defined and contentious. When it was first introduced in the 1980s, it tended to refer to a vague sense of responsibility for guiding the curriculum and programs in the school as an add-on to the more traditional managerial tasks. As it evolved, it took on many meanings, depending on how it was attached to other aspects of the school improvement agenda. Thus, for some, instructional leadership meant coaching and modeling quality teaching and thus a deep knowledge of subject matter (Stein & Nelson, 2003), which reflected a growing sense that the rigor of the curriculum needed more attention. For others, it meant creating decision making that focuses on student assessments (Halverson, Grigg, Prichett, & Thomas, 2005; Stiggins & Duke, 2008), which signaled the need for everyone in the school to focus on student outcomes. Still others saw it as developing denser networks of relationships among teachers that could focus on instruction and practice—in other words, creating communities of practice and collaboration (Spillane & Louis, 2002). All three have been shown to be important for school improvement.

Complexity and Shared Leadership

All of these expectations were added to the existing job of the school principal (none were taken away) which, not surprisingly, has resulted in increasing calls for distributed leadership by sharing improvement responsibilities more broadly and also by the development of an increased number of formal teacher-leader coaching roles that are often focused on instructional improvement and data use (McCombs & Marsh, 2009). In a world that used to consist almost only of a principal and teachers (with, perhaps, assistant principals in larger schools), there are now a large number of nonsupervisory leadership roles that are viewed as critical to the improvement agenda and an increasing number of district-based experts whose primary job is to work within schools on improvement issues (Camburn, Rowan, & Taylor, 2003). While leadership research still emphasizes the role of the principal, most principals work with multiple teams of leaders, each of which has a role to play in the larger job of increasing instructional quality while reducing between-classroom variation in student learning.

Much of this change has emerged as a response to external pressures, but some of the differentiated staffing and pressures toward instructional leadership have relatively deep roots in recommendations for educational reform. Just because they are well-accepted does not, however, mean that they are well understood or that their leadership roles are clear. Coaches are often poorly trained and given little support (Blarney, Meyer, & Sharon, 2008)—they are expected to support professional learning but cry out for more clarity and professional development for themselves (Rapacki & Francis, 2014). The meaning of instructional leadership and what it entails is also still unclear, although virtually all principal preparation programs cover the topic, and most principals are evaluated on whether they are doing it. The role of principals as coaches and supporters of teacher development is also confounded by new legislation that requires them to step up their evaluative functions—it is difficult to both coach and prepare to terminate a less effective teacher.

Focusing Leadership on Professional Learning

There is no easy solution to the dilemmas and pressures outlined above. The position that I take in this chapter is that the primary function of school leadership (in addition to ensuring effective management of core functions that ensure that learning can take place) is *to develop the school as a learning organization*. While this perspective will not eliminate the challenges that face administrators and teacher leaders, it does help to keep a focus on what needs to be done to improve schools: creating a culture that lives up to the Learning Forward belief statements:

1. Professional learning that improves educator effectiveness is fundamental to student learning.

2. All educators have an obligation to improve their practice.

3. More students achieve when educators assume collective responsibility for student learning.

4. Successful leaders create and sustain a culture of learning.

5. Effective school systems commit to continuous improvement for all adults and students. (Learning Forward, 2015)

INTEGRATION

ORGANIZING A SCHOOL AROUND LEARNING FOR ALL[2]

Where there is much desire to learn, there of necessity will be much arguing, much writing, many opinions; for opinion in good men is but knowledge in the making.

—John Milton[3]

Before I describe the specific ways in which school leaders can create an organizational learning culture, it is important to identify what is meant by organizational learning and what cultural features are needed to support it—in other words, to provide an integrated center to the discussion of leadership. This section treats features of the school's learning environment that are covered in the other Learning Forward standards (such as the characteristics of professional learning communities and the specific resources) only briefly but focuses on three features of leadership focus that are central to organizational learning.

First—Leaders Must Focus on the Details of the School's Daily Work NOT on Tests or Big Data

Some time ago, Chris Argyris noted that professionals in schools were "programmed" to ignore new information that challenged their existing practices, and with this observation he identified a central problem for improving schools: How do we get people to pay attention? (Argyris, 1976). In contrast to Argyris's focus on how individuals learn (or don't) in a school setting, other authors point to the role of social processes and structures that foster innovative thinking. While this may include data (see Learning Forward standard on data), the definition of information that leads to adaptive change is usually broader and includes (1) local expertise, (2) informal needs sensing, and (3) shared experiences (Kruse & Louis, 2009; Levitt & March, 1988)—"real" knowledge that is often left out of current cries to analyze testing information to improve student outcomes. Thus, organizational learning is usually distinguished from an immediate application of a particular type of information and is distinct from the current emphasis on data-driven decision making.

Table 1.1 summarizes some of the differences among the major terms that are often used in conjunction with professional learning. It is essential to emphasize that these are *not* competing perspectives: An effective leader of professional learning should not choose one but consider how each of them might affect the way in which they may be combined in any initiative under consideration. In particular, even if a leader wishes to develop a school in which all adults see themselves as learners, there will still always be a need to make sure that the right data are available and that there is a system to assess whether clearly defined new practices are being used.

One additional consequence, however, is that effective leadership of professional learning means that a school first needs to know where it stands. If a change or innovation in school practices is expected to

Table 1.1 Approaches to Professional Learning

	Stimulus: Why Knowledge Is Needed	Nature of Knowledge	Nature of Professional Learning and Cognitive Focus
Data-Based Decision Making	A specified issue/problem that requires a decision	Available information, usually statistical in nature	Professionals become habituated to including and prioritizing available databases in identifying problems and making decisions (Spillane, 2012).
Implementation	A specific program or set of new practices is to be used	Typically, written information, support materials, and training	Professionals learn specific skills that are incorporated as part of larger practice. There are standards for effective performance of new skills (Penuel, Fishman, Yamaguchi, & Gallagher, 2007).
Organizational Learning	Continuous efforts to improve professional practice	Knowledge comes from various sources	Learning is a group process that involves searching for and engaging with new information to improve current routines and develop new ones (Schechter, 2008).

emerge as a result of continuous improvement and incremental decisions rather than efforts to implement a new program, both the formal administrator and other school leaders need to know whether the school's professional staff has a mindset toward continuous improvement. This does not mean simply the absence of yellowed work sheets on student desks, and it is clearly not confined to the implementation of a particular practice or approach. Studies of organizational learning in fields ranging from public administration to health care emphasize assessing the *capacity for learning,* which reflects the presence of organizational *processes*, rather than particular outcomes or events (Marks & Louis, 1999; Marks, Louis, & Printy, 2002).

In order to understand a school's capacity for learning, school leaders need to adopt the eye of an anthropologist, looking for the details of how work is carried out. Typically, in this perspective, organizational learning can be identified by the presence of habituated *searching* for new information, *processing* and *evaluating* information with others, *incorporating* and *using* new ideas, and *generating ideas* within the organization as well as importing them from outside (Louis & Leithwood, 1998; Schechter, 2008). Looking for the signs of learning helps to provide an antidote to the popular image of schools as structurally rigid and unchanging and reminds staff that they already have many of the tools and mind-sets to become a learning organization. The central processes of organizational learning appear to provide a lever for changing schools and continuous improvement in innovative practice through frequent and deliberate adjustments of classroom practice in response to new ideas rather than major strategic reorientations (Brown & Duguid, 2001; Schechter & Qadach, 2012). Given the somewhat chaotic and rapidly changing environments faced by schools today, this approach to thoughtful, systematic but incremental improvements feels like a welcome return to professional practice rather than reform-managed-from-above. But you have to know what is happening and where.

Second—Leaders Must Actively Diagnose the School's Change Orientation

Among the outcomes of the organizational learning processes outlined above is a *change-orientation*: All school stakeholders are "actively seeking to improve both the content of and rate at which learning occurs" (Louis, 2006. p. 263) by being oriented toward group learning. In addition, continuous improvement culture assumes a *long-term commitment*, or the willingness and ability to see beyond the year-to-year fluctuations that schools typically encounter to stay in compliance with accountability requirements (Hallinger & Heck, 2011). Finally, as noted above, it assumes that organizational learning requires paying attention to *the implications of new information or knowledge for changes in practice,* including using quantitative or qualitative evidence as a basis for classroom and building decisions.

In sum, how would we know if a school was a learning organization? School leaders can look for the kinds of evidence suggested in Table 1.2:

Table 1.2   Are Schools Learning?

INDICATORS OF CAPACITY	Are most professionals in this school showing initiative to identify and solve problems? (*SEARCHING*)
	Are most professionals in this school seeking out and reading current findings in educational research? (*SEARCHING*)
	Are most professionals in this school sharing current findings in education with colleagues? (*SHARING*)
	After attending professional development activities this past year, are most professionals in this school sharing with other teachers in your school who did not attend the activity? (*COLLECTIVE EVALUATING*)
	After attending professional development activities this past year, are most professionals in this school sharing what they learned with administrators? (*COLLECTIVE EVALUATING*)
	Are most professionals in this school trying out new ideas from the above and discussing the results with their colleagues and administrators? (*USING AND RE-EVALUATING*)

Of course not all teachers engage in all of these practices every day. But if you cannot find evidence that most teachers are doing this regularly, then you may need to consider how to help people to pay attention to the new information and ideas that you are (I assume) discussing and reinforcing on a regular basis.

Third—Leaders Must Position Change Orientation in the Context of the Wider School Culture

These learning activities are more likely to occur in schools that have developed structures, cultures, and regular processes for supporting professional work and are more visible in some schools than others (Louis & Lee, 2014). According to Edgar Schein, a school culture reflects the group's consensus about how best to solve internal and external problems, but it is also "those elements of a group or organization that are most stable and least malleable" (Schein, 2010, p. 370). The collective mindset includes the "chunks" of shared knowledge, conceptual understandings that define their reality, and their learned and transmitted norms (Erickson, 1987). A school's history also gives meaning, sets guidelines for behavior, and helps groups to adapt to uncertain environments (Kruse & Louis, 2009). When school members are faced with the need to change, they must correspondingly adjust the beliefs that give meaning to their daily work lives, a generally slow process of adjustment and group learning that has been described as "organizational sensemaking" (Weick, 1995).

What school cultures are important for adapting and learning? Not surprisingly (and consistent with the Learning Forward standards), most studies find that organizational learning occurs either during or as a consequence of *collaborative communities of practice in the work context* (Lieberman, Miller, Roy, Hord, & Von Frank, 2014; Parise & Spillane, 2010). One study of adaptive work behavior found, for example, that "learning" (changing practices) occurred because people were simply "watching, noticing, trying and doing" (Tyre & von Hippel, 1997, p. 75). In schools, this may occur because of conversations with colleagues, observations by peers or administrators, feedback from students, reading, interactions with an expert coach, and other quasi-predictable activities (Camburn, 2010). Thus, group learning depends not only on processes but also shared norms such as collaboration, reflection, and willingness to try new things/ take collective risks. These can have a substantial impact on the ability of any organization to "manage" and make use of knowledge.

But other features of a school's culture in addition to collaboration are associated with organizational learning, and there is increasing consensus on those that may be particularly important. Recent research has integrated variables that are associated with student achievement across many studies and point to an increasing consensus about the cultural attributes of effective schools. A recent analysis of a large, national data set including schools from all parts of the United States, summarized in Table 1.3, suggests the following aspect of a school culture that may be particularly important for organizational learning behaviors:

Table 1.3 Attributes of Learning School Cultures

BEHAVIORAL INDICATORS	**IS IT SAFE TO ADAPT AND LEARN:** Do teachers trust each other? Do they trust their students? What about parents and the community? *(TRUST AND RESPECT)*
	IS THERE CONSENSUS AROUND LEARNING: Do teachers and principals authentically assess what students are learning and are able to do (in addition to test scores), and are expectations shared with students and parents? *(ACADEMIC PRESS)*
	IS THERE A FOCUS ON KNOWING INDIVIDUAL STUDENT NEEDS: Do teachers and principals know individual students well enough to tailor school work to their needs? Are resources allocated to students when they need them? *(STUDENT SUPPORT)*
	DO ALL TEACHERS SHARE RESPONSIBILITY FOR THE SUCCESS OF THE WHOLE SCHOOL: Do teachers focus their professional learning on the students and classes that they teach, or do they work on improving teaching and learning environments throughout? *(COLLECTIVE RESPONSIBILITY)*
	IS CURRENT PRACTICE OPEN AND SHARED? Do teachers and administrators share what they are doing—both strong and weak practices—with colleagues—including "walkthroughs" and longer observations of each other? *(DEPRIVATIZED PRACTICE)*
	DO DEEP CONVERSATIONS ABOUT LEARNING OCCUR REGULARLY? Do teachers and other professionals engage in regular and sustained conversations about what they are doing to improve? *(REFLECTIVE DIALOGUE)*

Of course these are not the only attributes of a school's culture that may indicate that it is a vibrant place for collective professional learning. However, before school leaders can begin the task of leading for learning, they must understand the features of their schools' cultures that may require attention if they are to be successful. Some strategies are discussed in each of the remaining sections, but other books provide more details about the general strategies for leading a school through a change process (Kotter, 2012; Kruse & Louis, 2009; Wagner et al., 2006).

To return to the quote from Milton at the beginning of this section, all of the above work can be done more or less behind the scenes. Integrative leadership, which means helping the school to recognize how it is currently learning and to prepare all of the members to increase their commitments to their own and their collective development as professionals, is a subtle set of tasks that involve observing, pulse taking, and a lot of talking to members. Because this underlying focus is on the people in the school and the school's culture, the next step is to understand the social architecture that must be developed as a support.

THE HUMAN DIMENSION OF PROFESSIONAL LEARNING

> *Intellectual growth should commence at birth and cease only at death.*
>
> —Albert Einstein[4]

School leaders who take professional learning seriously recognize that they are in an important business: talent development. This is not a perspective that is typically taught during administrator preparation programs, nor is it a focus that one often associates with the perspectives of district human resources departments. Yet creating learning schools requires that we pay attention to cultivating a learning orientation among teachers, particularly if the individuals in those groups are not ready to engage in collective reflective practice. The teachers and other professionals have many talents, but they need to be assessed, honed, and shared if professional learning is to become a core feature of the school's culture.

Before we begin thinking about leadership and the human dimension, it is important to interrogate the images about teachers and professional learning that we bring with us (Firestone, 1980; Morgan, 1997). Paavola, Lipponen, and Hakkarainen (2004) propose three useful metaphors of learning that have implications for leading: *acquisition, social participation, and knowledge creation.*

Acquisition: It Is Not About "Resistance to Change"

For many years, critics bemoaned the weak links between research and practice and posited the cause as resistance to change among teachers, which, coupled with lack of capacity, accounted for the poor performance of schools. A classic framework that challenged this assumption is the Concerns Based Adoption Model (Hall & Hord, 1987; Hall & Hord, 2001), usually referred to as CBAM. What the authors proposed was a developmental approach that linked individual concerns (typically about lack of capacity) with "levels of use" that were related to increasing understanding and confidence as a result of acquiring knowledge through practice. The continuing relevance of the CBAM model lies in its implications for helping individual teachers to acquire the knowledge and try the skills that support individual change (Anderson, 1997). School leaders need to understand where all teachers (or small groups of teachers) are on easily measureable "stages of concern" about any change that is occurring and the degree to which they have access to information that might help them take the next steps. As a practical tool for keeping track of major schoolwide innovations, it has weathered the test of time.

The limitation of CBAM is that it focuses on particular innovations, such as a new curriculum or instructional practice. In most schools today, the number of *known* new practices that are attempted simultaneously is mind boggling, and this does not take into consideration all of the adjustments and innovations that occur among smaller groups. An organizational learning model suggests that improved practices may come from many sources—external requirements or programs, internal examination of student work, or new ideas that are brought into the school community because a few teachers have attended a workshop.

In other words, the learning environment faced by today's school leaders is extremely complex. School leaders are not therapists: They have neither the time nor the training to address all of the factors in any teacher's world that might make him or her more or less likely to pay attention to learning opportunities. They must, however, as CBAM suggests, pay attention to what we know about willingness and capacity to learn.

Social Participation and Teacher Learning—What Do We Know?

Teachers who already feel good about their teaching are more open to learning about ways of getting even better (Camburn, 2010; De Neve, Devos, & Tuytens, 2015). Therein lies the problem for school leaders, who need to support those who are less secure in their teaching capacities rather than just hoping that the sprinters will encourage their slower colleagues to catch up. An approach that presumes individual learning has been the norm but is being supplanted by views that focus on the importance of relationships in creating richer learning environments for those who need more support. In particular, in other words, informal networks of sharing matter a great deal (Resnick & Scherrer, 2012), and they can be easily modeled by school leaders through more casual interactions as well as through more planned professional learning opportunities.

Teacher learning occurs most frequently when there is modest dissonance between what the individual believes and some knowledge or information that is easily available—or a dynamic tension between the status quo and intentional change (Printy & Marks, 2006). In other words, the sprinters—those that are far ahead and highly innovative—do not usually inspire those who need the most help in using new ideas. In many schools, however, even short but regular conversations among teachers and administrators about their professional learning are associated with greater willingness to look at the relevance of someone else's experience.

We know that teachers bring their prior experiences and beliefs about teaching into their initial jobs—and unless these are challenged, past mental models will determine future practice and learning (Senge, 2002). New ideas that challenge personal beliefs and values that are not well articulated cause teachers to retreat before engaging with them. There is also ample evidence that many adults learn best by seeing, doing, and reflecting rather than by reading and listening. Nonthreatening networks that develop because teachers and leaders are encouraged (or even required) to informally observe other classrooms may have many positive effects—including an increased propensity to talk about and try new practices (Ing, 2010; Zapeda, 2009). We also know that teachers are more likely to take up new ideas if they can see their connection to existing frames. This is problematic because "there is little consensus both within and between subject fields about what teachers need to know or how they need to know it" (Opfer & Pedder, 2011, p. 387). In education, like other settings, effective leaders are involved in helping all members of a school community to "make sense" of new ideas in the context of what is being done currently. In particular, when leaders directly or indirectly encourage teacher-to-teacher sharing, opportunities for creating consensus as well as challenging old beliefs increase (De Neve et al., 2015; Gallucci, 2008).

Effective school leaders are also storytellers who consistently weave together a larger picture of the innovations that are taking place in the school and how they can fit together. Stories are particularly useful as ways of exploring differences while creating consensus—as long as they are not instructional in their focus but open-ended and dialogic. Thus, for example, a school leader who tells a story about how another school has integrated a controversial idea but emphasizes the journey and struggle rather than the final victory opens up opportunities for teachers to discuss their own and a group journey. Leaders do not have to make up stories themselves but can repeat stories that they hear from others to encourage reflection and discussion. When shared, stories have the power to solidify groups because they are a form of shared knowledge that conveys an understanding of "how the world works" or "how we do things around here" that does not demand a logical exposition or a handbook of rules.

Teacher Learning and Knowledge Creation

We typically think of teachers as users of knowledge acquired through various professional learning opportunities, but it is important to remember that teachers also create new ideas and programs. A popular book such as *Teach Like a Champion* is, after all, a compilation of the effective teaching strategies that the author observed and not the result of a research project (Lemov, 2015). One of the most popular federally funded knowledge sharing programs of the 1970s through the 1990s was the National Diffusion Network, where the "knowledge base" consisted of programs that were often developed by teachers; today, teachers take advantage of social sharing sites like Pinterest and other online communities to share their work.

Effective school leaders often simply expect teachers to take on the role of knowledge creation and build this into their job-embedded professional development plans. Teacher knowledge creation goes beyond inventing new teaching strategies that work: Action research, carried out well, can generate energy for reform that moves beyond a few individual classrooms (Paavola et al., 2004). School leaders can encourage shared knowledge development (which obviously has more impact on the whole school than a brilliant teacher in a single classroom) with very small nonmonetary rewards—supporting a group's trip to get more information, providing time to explain an action research project to the entire staff, or, as in the case of one school that I studied many years ago, supporting teachers in developing a local conference to showcase the results of teachers-as-inventors (Louis & Kruse, 1998).

Acknowledging the creative side of teaching does not privilege professional knowledge over research knowledge or data. All forms of knowledge are important to professional learning, but the well-established principle of sustained, disciplined "tinkering" is central to creating a learning organization. Continuous improvement models derived from industry require translation to be useful in schools (Detert, Louis, & Schroeder, 2001), but we must trust the collective capacity of teachers to address quality through shared invention.

Talent Development in Schools

In the past, professional development was often confused with talent development, but the concepts are quite different. Professional development in schools has traditionally been synonymous with training (either orientation to or preparing for specific new skills) provided to individuals or work groups, often under the assumption that "a teacher is a teacher is a teacher." Talent development requires thinking more broadly about the human capital in the school, focusing on *professional learning for each person and the group as a whole given where they are at any moment.*

What does attention to the human side of professional learning mean for the broader question of developing a school's capacity for improvement? First, there must be an "architecture" to any talent development model that acknowledges both individual and social characteristics of the teachers and other leaders in the school. The first step is, therefore, some diagnosis of the capacities of the people who are already there, while the second step is coming to some agreement within the school on what kinds of talents are most important for moving forward. Then school leaders, along with others in the school, need to address designing recruitment/retention strategies, development approaches, and rewards that will help to move the school forward. This requires understanding the differences that underlie the agreed upon definitions of needed talent.

What newer teachers need is not usually the same as what more experienced teachers need—but they may have different kinds of expertise that each can contribute to the other. Any given department or grade-level team may have strong expertise in some areas but may be weaker in others. Finally, groups may have greater or lesser capacities for working well together on professional learning, which means that a one-size-fits-all approach may not work after an initial orientation.

Diagnosis points to the implied hierarchy in the perspective outlined above. Leaders cannot begin to support teachers-as-knowledge-creators in a school where most of the teachers are relatively weak or are dispirited. The foundation, as indicated above, lies in increasing self-efficacy, which, in some cases, may initially rest on the school leader's capacity to provide effective feedback that affirms what is important and what needs to be changed. This presumes, of course, instructional leadership capacity to model and coach, whether provided by the principal or others. In a school where quite a few teachers have realistic and positive assessments of their capacity to improve, instructional leadership that helps to develop knowledge-sharing networks that focus on student learning may be most important. The value of networks lies in how frequently they are used to stimulate teachers to see and share ideas that create a more cohesive collective image of quality. Only schools that have established learning environments may be ready to encourage and support inventors.

But again—developing the human side also means paying a great deal of attention to the underlying architecture that supports effective professional learning. High teacher turnover, weak recruitment strategies, the absence of established ways of socializing new members, and a weak connection between individual professional learning goals and broader school improvement goals can undermine a learning culture very quickly. In other words, management as well as leadership of the human side of the school still demands attention to create effective professional learning.

CARING AND EMOTIONAL INTELLIGENCE

The key, central to care theory, is this: caring-about (or, perhaps a sense of justice) must be seen as instrumental in establishing the conditions under which caring-for can flourish.

—Nel Noddings[5]

The previous section focused on human relationships and professional learning in schools but doesn't fully address what school leaders can do to foster them. The CBAM work draws attention to an aspect of learning and change that is imperative: Leaders must become adept at managing the emotional side of their schools, which includes the emotions associated with dissonance and change. For nearly 25 years, traditional research about the importance of leadership intelligence—the capacity to analyze and solve problems—has been balanced by the idea of leader emotional intelligence—the capacity to understand and support individuals and the group (George, 2000; Hargreaves, 2002).

Emotional intelligence is important in all work settings, but there is some evidence that one aspect of the emotional life of schools is particularly important: caring. Philosopher Nel Noddings is, perhaps, the most frequently cited author supporting an ethic of care as the heart of teaching (Noddings, 1992), but many in both education and other human service professions argue that motivating individual professionals and effective group work requires maintaining a laser-like focus on caring as a central value. In particular, like other human services professionals, teacher identity is grounded in a sense of values that have emotional and personal resonance (Geijsel & Meijers, 2005), among which is the focus on the professional responsibility that teachers and school leaders assume for nurturing the next generation.

Emotional Intelligence and Professional Learning

Current leadership research suggests that guiding a learning organization toward a specific goal requires two kinds of leadership: transformational (focusing on the tasks of developing vision and driving a group toward a new future) and transactional (focusing on the nature of relationships and interactions between leaders and others in the school) (Vera & Crossan, 2004). As most experienced educational leaders know, maintaining a high functioning school requires constant attention to both strategic direction and the current needs of students, teachers, parents, and others. Emotional intelligence focuses on the transactional, under the assumption that unless the human side is working well, transformation cannot occur. Understanding what it takes for school leaders to work with the needs of others has been crystallized in the idea of emotionally intelligent leadership.

But attending to the needs of others does not always produce a strong culture of professional learning in a school. A principal may, for example, be empathetic and effective in working with students or in mediating disagreements among members without stimulating teachers to search for, share, experiment with, and use new ideas. Research increasingly suggests that some kinds of behaviors associated with emotional intelligence are also associated with creativity and learning. School leaders must become more adept at analyzing and working with the emotional side of teachers' work if they are to create dynamic learning environments, and they must focus on the emotions that support or get in the way of adult learning. Huy's (2011) work on emotional intelligence and organizational creativity provides an important clue that is easily translated into a school setting. Table 1.4 connects five tasks of

Table 1.4   Emotionally Intelligent Leadership and Professional Learning

Emotional Leadership Task	Professional Learning Work
Collective goal development	*Learning goals must be treated as dynamic.* Underlying issues and concerns are viewed as "part of the process" as goals are refined.
Appreciation of work	*Leaders need to understand the details of the learning work.* They should demonstrate understanding of the inherent stressors involved with teaching as a caring profession; relieving unreasonable burdens associated with change and learning is critical.
Generating enthusiasm, cooperation, and trust	*Leaders need to take care of emotional bonds.* Change and learning may fray previously agreed upon understanding; disagreements need to be addressed and accepted as part of the learning process.
Flexibility	*Leaders need to take the pulse of learning challenges.* "Backing off" may be appropriate; acceptance of risk and small failures will encourage more learning; acceptance of individual differences in the level of challenge and rate of change is critical.
Identity and meaning	*Leaders need to be passionate about the values underlying goals.* Learning is motivated by available opportunities to enact school and professional values in everyday work.

emotional leadership that he identified in a private sector organization (Huy, 2011) to the task of professional learning in schools.

Teachers assess the effectiveness of their school leaders by observing their behavior and not by measuring intentions. School leaders may claim that they appreciate the work of teachers, but if they do not participate in at least some of teachers' development experiences, teachers will not be convinced that they have a deep understanding of what is required of them as they move into deep changes in their classroom practices. Similarly, school leaders who espouse the need for a learn-experiment-assess-learn cycle, but acknowledge only successful changes, will not be taken seriously as emotionally competent leaders.

Perhaps most importantly, leaders must balance their personal commitments to particular school projects with the need to support the motivating passions of others, which may mean, on occasion, acknowledging the variety and occasional incompatibility among the professional values and motivations that teachers bring to their work. Leaders who do not genuinely understand, for example, the tension between a teacher's love of his or her content and the changes needed in order to create culturally relevant learning experiences will have less influence than those who balance the aspiration (more cultural relevance) with an understanding of the emotional loss (giving up content that has value to the teacher). Lack of attention to this balance may create chaos that diminishes learning (Huy, 2002).

Obtaining a balance is difficult: Leaders must be genuinely and deeply committed to the learning and change work. Unless members of the school community believe that leaders prioritize learning of particular kinds and participate in the learning themselves, their advocacy will be perceived as counterfeit. On the other hand, leaders must also recognize that their values and hopes are part of the larger stew of emotional responses to demands for change, and that they are responsible for being focused on and understanding of others.

Caring Leadership for Professional Learning[6]

Caring is only one aspect of emotional leadership, but it is particularly important in schools and other human service organizations. Without compassion and caring, leaders cannot understand and respond to the felt discomfort of teachers' experienced reality: Some students do not do well in spite of a teacher's best efforts, and others bring problems or issues that teachers do not know how to handle. The best teachers I know go home every day with both a sense of gratitude and success and an awareness that they could have done better in explaining something, handling a classroom disagreement, or working with a student who was disruptive. The centrality of caring as an aspect of addressing the emotional pain that is ever present in schools is, therefore, pivotal.

There are clearly many specific leadership behaviors that are associated with caring, but the problem for school leaders is that *there is no simple list of what they should do to demonstrate caring.* The absence of checklists (in contrast to the much touted behavioral approaches to effective teaching) is actually logical. Each professional group varies in the way in which caring would be expressed: Nursing has little in common with teaching in terms of the day-to-day challenges faced at work, while the issues facing high-poverty secondary schools may be quite different from those that affect affluent elementary schools. As a consequence, the number of different situations that confront leaders and demand emotionally caring responses is virtually infinite. Lists will not help.

However, we can assume that a school leader's efforts to promote professional and organizational learning will be gauged by whether he or she meets the underlying criteria of caring. We may not be able to create a simple map of emotionally intelligent and caring responses, but no teacher will find themselves at a loss to answer whether a leader's reaction to any given situation is more or less caring and compassionate. Several conditions that define caring and compassionate leader behavior include the following (Boyatzis, Smith, & Blaize, 2006; Louis, Murphy, & Smylie, 2016; Noddings, 2005):

1. What school leaders do is based on authentic knowledge and understanding of the cared-for.

2. What school leaders do is based on and developed out of attentiveness to the cared-for.

3. The caring actions of school leaders are motivated by aspirations for the success and personal well-being of the cared-for.

4. Where possible, the school leaders' caring is recognized and acknowledged by the ones cared-for.

In a recent study, I identified a number of characteristics of caring behaviors among school leaders. Teachers who stated that their school leaders engaged in any one of these behaviors were very likely to be positive about the others as well. What this means is that teachers have a general perception of their school leader as either more or less caring. Examinations of teacher interviews in the same schools indicated that teachers in some schools spontaneously described their principal in similar terms that indicated caring—which in others they did not.

The important point about these behaviors is that they had a big impact on organizational learning (as defined in Table 1.2). *Teachers who described their principals as exhibiting caring behaviors also indicated that they and their colleagues actively searched for and used information to improve their practices.*

Principal caring had other effects as well: Teachers in schools with caring leaders were more likely to describe high levels of collaboration with their colleagues and were more likely to visit each other's classrooms and discuss instruction. In other words,

Table 1.5   Sample Caring Behaviors That Are Linked With Organizational Learning

TRUST	My school administrator develops an atmosphere of caring and trust.
	If my principal promised to do something, he or she would follow through.
SITUATIONALITY	My school administrator is supportive of my decisions about managing student discipline problems.
	When teachers are struggling, our principal provides support for them.
AUTHENTICITY	My school administrator ensures wide participation in decisions about school improvement.
	In general, I believe my principal's motives and intentions are good.
ATTENTIVENESS	My principal is responsive to the needs and concerns expressed by community members.
SELFLESS MOTIVATION	I feel free to discuss work problems with my principal without fear of having it used against me later.

Figure 1.2   Caring School Leadership and Organizational Learning

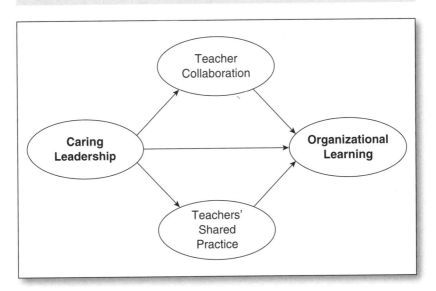

they saw their schools as socially connected and safe places to engage in informal professional learning. Both of these also affect organizational learning. The overall relationship between caring and organizational learning is shown in Figure 1.2.

Caring has additional effects that are important in the school context. In particular, in schools where teachers view their principals as caring, they are also more likely to report that the school has an ethos that supports the development of all students. This goes beyond the general mantra that "all students can and will learn" to more concrete observations about equitable school practices that support students' academic work, such as ensuring that all students have an equal opportunity to be assigned to the best teachers and ensuring that students who need extra help always get it. In other words, teachers who feel cared for by their principal are also more likely to support and help institutionalize school practices that provide caring and equitable environments for student learning.

Revisiting Emotions and Professional Learning

Individuals and groups continually manage and organize themselves on the basis of their emotional responses to organizational issues as well as on the basis of avoiding emotion, and that both of these have strategic implications. (Vince, 2001, p. 79)

Vince (2001) suggests an important point of departure for considering the active role of school leaders in managing the emotions that may impede professional learning. What principal is not aware of the resisters and the sprinters among the teachers—informal groups that organize themselves around emotional responses to learning opportunities? One of the most adept principals I have known always organized initial learning groups by including at least one resister in every team. While not a strategy that works universally, it ensured that the sprinters had the responsibility of engaging with their skeptical colleagues and that the skeptics were listened to respectfully. The principal didn't have to manage the emotions associated with "let's do it right now" and "no way" because he delegated that to the teachers. In each school, there may be ways for both teacher leaders and administrators to ensure that the micro-architecture of learning groups increases rather than decreases opportunities for genuine discussion of emotions.

What teachers need most is a feeling of safety in professional learning. The easiest way to avoid emotions is to avoid situations in which fear of failure, of disrupting a system that is working (even if suboptimally), or conflict might arise. Yet the avoidance of emotionally challenging environments in school does nothing to foster a genuine learning community among those who may need it most. Thus, school leaders' first steps in developing a culture for organizational learning is to be the first to admit what they don't know and then create safe places where the fear of appearing incompetent is minimized, and the professional reluctance to discuss value differences can be overcome.

Professional learning can be both exciting and uncomfortable in a context where everything seems to be changing all of the time. Once the architecture for an effective learning community has been put in place—recruitment, overall development strategies, and rewards—leaders must turn to the inevitable problem of managing the individual and group emotions that are involved in learning. Teachers understand learning environments for children but typically do not have a good grasp of how these may translate into effective learning environments for adults. These may be heightened when teachers become engaged in work that requires deeper group reflection. The underlying principles of group and organizational learning, which require confronting and discussing differences that will stimulate (or increase) unstated feelings related to professional competence and performance are less familiar, and teachers who may be brilliant in managing classroom emotions may be less competent in settings with peers. Both emotional intelligence and deep commitment to developing a caring culture in the school are fundamental to building a learning school.

LEARNING TO BE A LEARNING ORGANIZATION

Effective professional learning communities do not just happen because we convene or assign educators into groups of learners. They take focused effort to build and sustain.

—Killion & Roy[7]

We have all seen or heard of leaders who are very effective in one school (sometimes even as a "turnaround" guru) but who are flustered and apparently ineffective when they are transferred to another school where they have difficulty working with a different group of teachers. Why does this happen? New leaders can exacerbate fears that were already present; they may stir up resentment if a previous principal was well liked because teachers were left alone; they may have inadvertently offended an influential teacher with actions that would, in their previous schools, be viewed as legitimate or even caring. Under these and other circumstances, developing a strong culture of professional learning may seem impossible. Yet, these are the settings in which leadership for professional learning may be most called for.

Shirley M. Hord's chapter in this book addresses the specifics of what leaders can and should do to help create a dynamic environment for professional learning. Here, I propose a framework for thinking about how schools can learn to become communities of collaborative adult learners, which focuses on the building blocks that leaders can put into place.[8] The three basic elements are pictured in Figure 1.3 as the base of a pyramid: All three are essential if a school is to become a place where professional learning is the air that teachers breathe every day. When all three are in balance, the apex of the figure suggests that a learning organization will result.

Figure 1.3   The Learning Organization

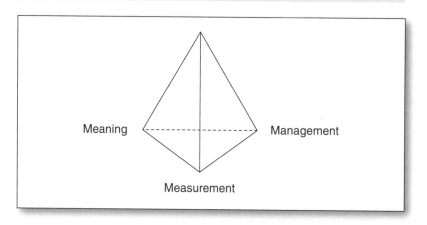

Of course there is no final "Eureka! We are a learning organization" moment, but it does not take advanced solid geometry to note that if any side of the pyramid erodes, the entire pyramid will collapse.

Meaning: What Does My School Mean by Professional Learning?

Before a school leader can begin to strengthen the school's commitment to professional learning, there must first be some emergent consensus about what the idea means. If some teachers are stuck in ideas about professional learning that were generated from bad experiences with being herded into an auditorium to listen to the newest state regulations regarding the management of student medications, a leadership group's enthusiasm for developing learning communities is unlikely to motivate. On the other hand, if there is a small group of teachers that has traditionally had access to the school's travel fund to feed their own interests, they may be reluctant to give up a privileged position. Perhaps worst is the school where a previous principal mandated professional learning communities along with specific tasks to be accomplished, leading to a strong sense that learning means following an administratively designated path. Thus, the first step must be to establish consistent ways of *communicating* about professional learning, while the second is to engage the entire staff in *developing a definition* of professional learning that reflects the commitment of at least most teachers and reinforces professionalism and collective efficacy. As part of that work, classroom teachers, coaches, and administrators must also agree on attributes or characteristics of a learning school. While some of the activity around meaning-making can and should be generated within the group, there are many short readings or handouts that could stimulate discussion (see, for example, Killion & Roy, 2009).

Meaning must be translated into action, of course. Part of the discussion of meaning will necessarily focus on what people think they want to do and are able to do. The meaning-making process will, if it goes well, result in some commitments that will be reflected in individual teacher development plans and also in the group's commitment to sharing and collaborating in a movement toward becoming a learning school.

Measurement: Are We Doing What We Say We Want?

Every school leader knows that groups pay most attention to any aspect of their work that is reviewed. It is not necessary to design extensive evaluation systems to determine a school's progress toward becoming a learning organization, but it is almost imperative that some energy be devoted to *assessing* progress. This could be as simple as a short survey that asks teachers to rate how well the school is doing based on the Learning Forward standards, followed by a discussion of what is working well and what needs to be improved. The purpose here is not to develop a defensible public metric but to keep the indicators of professional learning (supplemented by some that may reflect the school as a learning organization) in the front of teachers' minds on an annual basis.

The assessment process should become part of a routine reflection on what needs to be adjusted in order to achieve the agreed upon ideals of becoming a group of committed professional learners. That reflection will, if incorporated into staff and group meetings, result in reshaping both meaning (definitions and expectations) and any action commitments for the future.

Management: Professional Learning and Herding Cats

Leading a group of education professionals in the direction of enhanced professional learning is not a simple task. Individual learning is still extremely important, and the path to organizational learning is not straightforward and concrete. Nevertheless, in order to reach a goal of embedded professional learning that is connected with larger school goals, school leaders must become vigilant in keeping tabs on emergent accelerator ideas as well monitoring the potholes. This is particularly true because moving individual professional learning into the sphere of shared learning requires being observant about new prospects rather than following a well-defined strategic plan. In other words, managing lies at the core of making sure that the work of meaning-making and measuring professional learning is well-guided (see Figure 1.4).

Professional learning opportunities arise unexpectedly and in many places: Someone sees a new indicator of the school's performance, a group of teachers and a coach locate a problem with student learning that requires focused attention, or a highly relevant speaker's schedule appears in someone's inbox at the last minute. Yet, good school leadership requires keeping all eyes on an agreed upon target or long-range goals for the school, in which professional learning is a both a means and an end in itself. Learning keeps professionals energized and excited, but leaders must ensure that all

Figure 1.4 Meaning, Measuring, Managing in Professional Learning

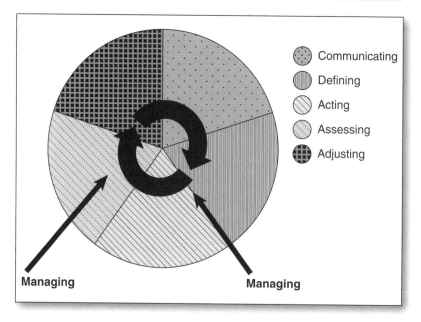

eyes are regularly (re)directed toward the target. Balancing energy and focus requires a great deal of day-to-day attention to the details. In the case of professional learning for individuals and the school as a whole, nothing can replace the role of "management by walking about" and talking to people. In today's larger and more complex schools, as I noted earlier, no principal can do all of this work by himself or herself: He or she must rely on other formal and informal leaders to both find potential problems and to carry the message about how and what to share from individual learning.

Professional learning and organizational learning rely on communication, and unless the leaders in the school model its value, people will choose to work largely by themselves or with a few trusted colleagues. Leaders who do not consistently and publicly reflect on their own learning process and share their own learning stories will not demonstrate the challenging reality of professional learning to others. Nor can leaders of schools that already have an engaged learning environment afford to back off on the tasks of gathering, sorting, and modeling learning: Excellence in professional learning is not self-sustaining but requires vigilant focus on the learning that is happening now and its connections with the established focus for school improvement. Leaders cannot single-handedly create a learning school, but without their engaged guidance, one will rarely emerge and even more rarely be sustained.

NOTES

1. Quote prepared for the speech, to be given in Dallas, TX, in 1963.
2. This section draws on previous work (Louis & Lee, 2014).
3. Milton, J. (1643). *The aeropagitica.* Retrieved from http://www.stlawrence institute.org/vol14mit.html
4. Einstein, A. (n.d.). *BrainyQuote.com.* Retrieved from http://www.brainy quote.com
5. Noddings, N. (2002). *Starting at home: Caring and social policy.* Berkeley: University of California Press, p. 23.
6. My focus on caring leadership is influenced by Murphy, J., & Torre, D. (2015). *Creating productive cultures in schools for students, teachers, and parents.* Thousand Oaks, CA: Corwin, and by ongoing work with Joe Murphy and Mark Smylie (Louis, Murphy, & Smylie, 2016; Smylie, Murphy, & Louis, in press). Parts of this section draw on Louis, Murphy, and Smylie (2016).

7. Killion, J., & Roy, P. (2009). *Becoming a learning school.* Oxford, OH: National Staff Development Council, p. 3.
8. This figure has been adapted from Campbell & Cairns (1994).

REFERENCES

Anderson, S. E. (1997). Understanding teacher change: Revisiting the concerns based adoption model. *Curriculum Inquiry, 27*(3), 331–367.

Argyris, C. (1976). Theories of action that inhibit individual learning. *American Psychologist, 31*(9), 638.

Blarney, K. L., Meyer, C. K., & Sharon, W. (2008). Middle and high school literacy coaches: A national survey. *Journal of Adolescent & Adult Literacy, 52*(4), 310–323.

Boyatzis, R. E., Smith, M. L., & Blaize, N. (2006). Developing sustainable leaders through coaching and compassion. *Academy of Management Learning & Education, 5*(1), 8–24.

Brown, J. S., & Duguid, P. (2001). Knowledge and organization: A social-practice perspective. *Organization Science, 12*(2), 198–213.

Camburn, E. M. (2010). Embedded teacher learning opportunities as a site for reflective practice: An exploratory study. *American Journal of Education, 116*(4), 463–489.

Camburn, E. M., Rowan, B., & Taylor, J. E. (2003). Distributed leadership in schools: The case of elementary schools adopting comprehensive school reform models. *Educational Evaluation and Policy Analysis, 25*(4), 347–373.

Campbell, T., & Cairns, H. (1994). Developing and measuring the learning organization. *Industrial and Commercial Training, 7*(26), 10–15.

De Neve, D., Devos, G., & Tuytens, M. (2015). The importance of job resources and self-efficacy for beginning teachers' professional learning in differentiated instruction. *Teaching and Teacher Education, 47*, 30–41.

Detert, J., Louis, K. S., & Schroeder, R. (2001). A culture framework for education: Defining quality values for U.S. high schools. *Journal of School Effectiveness and School Improvement, 12*(2), 183.

Erickson, F. (1987). Conceptions of school culture: An overview. *Educational Administration Quarterly, 23*(4), 11–24.

Fink, L. D. (2013). *Creating significant learning experiences: An integrated approach to designing college courses.* New York, NY: Wiley.

Firestone, W. A. (1980). Images of schools and patterns of change. *American Journal of Education, 88*(4), 459–487.

Gallucci, C. (2008). Districtwide instructional reform: Using sociocultural theory to link professional learning to organizational support. *American Journal of Education, 114*(4), 541–581.

Geijsel, F., & Meijers, F. (2005). Identity learning: The core process of educational change. *Educational Studies, 31*(4), 419–430.

George, J. M. (2000). Emotions and leadership: The role of emotional intelligence. *Human Relations, 53*(8), 1027–1055.

Grissom, J., & Loeb, S. (2011). Triangulating principal effectiveness: How perspectives of parents, teachers, and assistant principals identify the central importance of managerial skills. *American Educational Research Journal, 48*(5), 1091–1123.

Guskey, T. R. (2003). Analyzing lists of the characteristics of effective professional development to promote visionary leadership. *NASSP Bulletin, 87*(637), 4–20.

Hall, G. E., & Hord, S. M. (1987). *Change in schools: Facilitating the process* Albany, NY: SUNY Press.

Hall, G. E., & Hord, S. M. (2001). *Implementing change: Patterns, principles, and potholes.* Boston, MA: Allyn and Bacon.

Hallinger, P., & Heck, R. H. (2011). Exploring the journey of school improvement: Classifying and analyzing patterns of change in school improvement processes and learning outcomes. *School Effectiveness and School Improvement, 22*(1), 1–27.

Hallinger, P., & Murphy, J. F. (1986). The social context of effective schools. *American Journal of Education, 94*(3), 328–355.

Halverson, R., Grigg, J., Prichett, R., & Thomas, C. (2005). The new instructional leadership: Creating data-driven instructional systems in schools. *Journal of School Leadership, 17*(2), 159–194.

Hargreaves, A. (2002). The emotional geographies of teaching. *Teachers College Record, 103*(6), 1056–1080.

Heckman, P. E., Oakes, J., & Sirotnik, K. A. (1983). Expanding the concepts of school renewal and change. *Educational Leadership, 40*(7), 26–32.

Horng, E., & Loeb, S. (2010). New thinking about instructional leadership. *The Phi Delta Kappan, 92*(3), 66–69. doi: 10.2307/25753685

Huy, Q. N. (2002). Emotional balancing of organizational continuity and radical change: The contribution of middle managers. *Administrative Science Quarterly, 47*(1), 31–69.

Huy, Q. N. (2011). How middle managers' group-focus emotions and social identities influence strategy implementation. *Strategic Management Journal, 32*(13), 1387–1410.

Ing, M. (2010). Using informal classroom observations to improve instruction. *Journal of Educational Administration, 48*(3), 337–358.

Ingersoll, R. M., Hoxby, C. M., & Scrupski, A. F. (2004). Why some schools have more underqualified teachers than others. *Brookings Papers on Education Policy, 7*, 45–88.

Killion, J. (1999). *What works in the middle: Results-based staff development.* Oxford, OH: National Staff Development Council.

Killion, J., & Roy, P. (2009). *Becoming a learning school*. Oxford, OH: National Staff Development Council.

Kotter, J. P. (2012). *Leading Change*. Boston, MA: Harvard Business School Press.

Kruse, S. D., & Louis, K. S. (2009). *Strong cultures: A school leader's guide to change*. Thousand Oaks, CA: Corwin.

Learning Forward. (2011). *Standards for professional learning*. Oxford, OH: Learning Forward.

Learning Forward. (2015). *Vision, mission, beliefs, priorities*. Retrieved from http://learningforward.org/who-we-are/purpose-beliefs-priorities#.Vtys2Y-cGUl

Lemov, D. (2015). *Teach like a champion 2.0: 62 Techniques That Put Students on the Path to College*. San Francisco, CA: Jossey Bass.

Levitt, B., & March, J. G. (1988). Organizational learning. *American Review of Sociology, 14*, 319–340.

Lieberman, A., Miller, L., Roy, P., Hord, S., & Von Frank, V. (2014). *Reach the highest standard in professional learning: Learning communities*. Thousand Oaks, CA: Corwin.

Louis, K. S. (2006). *Organizing for school change*. London and New York: Taylor and Francis.

Louis, K. S., & Kruse, S. D. (1998). Creating community in reform: Images of organizational learning in urban schools. In K. Leithwood & K. S. Louis (Eds.), *Organizational learning in schools* (pp. 17–46). New York, NY: Routledge.

Louis, K. S., & Lee, M. (2014). *Fostering organizational learning*. Paper presented at the International Congress for School Effectiveness and School Improvement, Yogyakarta, Indonesia.

Louis, K. S., & Leithwood, K. (1998). From organizational learning to professional learning communities. In K. Leithwood & K. S. Louis (Eds.), *Organizational learning in schools* (pp. 275–285). Lisse, NL: Swets and Zeitlinger.

Louis, K. S., Murphy, J., & Smylie, M. (2016). Caring leadership in schools: Findings from exploratory analyses. *Educational Administration Quarterly 52* (2) 310-348.

Marks, H. M., & Louis, K. S. (1999). Teacher empowerment and the capacity for organizational learning. *Educational Administration Quarterly, 35*(4), 751–781.

Marks, H. M., Louis, K. S., & Printy, S. (2002). The capacity for organizational learning: Implications for pedagogy and student achievement. In K. Leithwood (Ed.), *Organizational learning and school improvement*. Greenwich, CT: JAI.

McCombs, J. S., & Marsh, J. A. (2009). Lessons for boosting the effectiveness of reading coaches. *The Phi Delta Kappan, 90*(7), 501–507. doi: 10.2307/20446160

Morgan, G. (1997). *Images of organization* (2nd ed.). Thousand Oaks, CA: Sage.

Murphy, J., & Torre, D. (2015). *Creating productive cultures in schools: For students, teachers, and parents.* Thousand Oaks, CA: Corwin.

Noddings, N. (1992). *The challenge to care in schools: An alternative approach to education.* New York, NY: Teachers College Press.

Noddings, N. (2005). *The challenge to care in schools: An alternative approach to education* (2nd ed.). New York, NY: Teachers College Press.

Opfer, V. D., & Pedder, D. (2011). Conceptualizing teacher professional learning. *Review of educational research, 81*(3), 376–407.

Paavola, S., Lipponen, L., & Hakkarainen, K. (2004). Models of innovative knowledge communities and three metaphors of learning. *Review of Educational Research, 74*(4), 557–576.

Parise, L. M., & Spillane, J. P. (2010). Teacher learning and instructional change: How formal and on-the-job learning opportunities predict change in elementary school teachers' practice. *The Elementary School Journal, 110*(3), 323–346.

Penuel, W. R., Fishman, B. J., Yamaguchi, R., & Gallagher, L. P. (2007). What makes professional development effective? Strategies that foster curriculum implementation. *American Educational Research Journal, 44*(4), 921–958.

Printy, S. M., & Marks, H. M. (2006). Shared leadership for teacher and student learning. *Theory Into Practice, 45*(2), 125–132.

Rapacki, L. J., & Francis, D. I. C. (2014). I am a math coach: Now what? *Teaching Children Mathematics, 20*(9), 556–563.

Resnick, L. B., & Scherrer, J. (2012). Social networks in "nested learning organizations"—a commentary. *American Journal of Education, 119*(1), 183–192.

Rossmiller, R. (1992). The secondary school principal and teachers' quality of work life. *Educational Management and Administration, 20*(3), 132–146.

Schechter, C. (2008). Organizational learning mechanisms: The meaning, measure, and implications for school improvement. *Educational Administration Quarterly*, 155–186.

Schechter, C., & Qadach, M. (2012). Toward an organizational model of change in elementary schools: The contribution of organizational learning mechanisms. *Educational Administration Quarterly, 48*(1), 116–153. doi: 10.1177/0013161x11419653

Schein, E. H. (2010). *Organizational culture and leadership* (2nd ed.). San Francisco, CA: Jossey Bass.

Senge, P. (2002). *The fifth discipline: The art and practice of the learning organization.* New York, NY: Currency Doubleday.

Smylie, M., Murphy, J., & Louis, K. S. (2015). *Caring school leadership: A cross-disciplinary and cross-occupational framework.* Paper presented at the annual conference of the American Educational Research Association, Chicago, IL.

Spillane, J. (2012). Data in practice: Conceptualizing the data-based decision-making phenomena. *American Journal of Education, 118*(2), 113–141

Spillane, J., & Louis, K. S. (2002). School improvement processes and practices: Professional learning for building instructional capacity. In J. Murphy (Ed.), *Challenges of leadership: Yearbook of the National Society for the Study of Education.* Chicago, IL: University of Chicago Press.

Stein, M. K., & Nelson, B. S. (2003). Leadership content knowledge. *Educational Evaluation and Policy Analysis, 25*(4), 423–448.

Stiggins, R., & Duke, D. (2008). Effective instructional leadership requires assessment leadership. *The Phi Delta Kappan, 90*(4), 285–291.

Tyre, M. J., & von Hippel, E. (1997). The situated nature of adaptive learning in organizations. *Organization Science, 8*(1), 71–83.

Vera, D., & Crossan, M. (2004). Strategic leadership and organizational learning. *The Academy of Management Review, 29*(2), 222–240. doi: 10.2307/20159030

Vince, R. (2001). The impact of emotion on organizational learning. *Human Resource Development International, 5*(1), 73–85.

Wagner, T., Kegan, R., Lahey, L., Lemons, R., Garnier, J., Helsing, D., . . . Rassmussen, H. (2006). *Change leadership: A practical guide to transforming our schools.* San Francisco, CA: Jossey Bass.

Waller, W. (1932). *The sociology of teaching.* New York, NY: John Wiley & Sons.

Weick, K. (1995). *Sensemaking in organizations.* Thousand Oaks, CA: Sage.

Zapeda, S. J. (2009). *The instructional leader's guide to informal classroom observations.* New York, NY: Routledge.

CHAPTER TWO

Learning Together for Leading Together

Shirley M. Hord

*Ours is not the task of fixing the entire world all at once,
but of stretching out to mend the part of the world that is
within reach.*

—Clarissa Pinkola Estes

At 7:30 a.m. on a cold but bright and sunny winter day, Superintendent Homero McElroy met with his cabinet, the five
associate superintendents. The chief administrators of the district's
five area subdistricts included three males and two females, each of
whom had been awarded the PhD degree for their university studies.
This meeting in a small private dining room of the local eatery was
the regular twice-a-month gathering where the top-level district
administrators shared information, reviewed events, identified significant news, and—most important—reported concerns that derived
from their schools' staff members and from the community that the
campus and district staff served.

"Thanks for being here today, colleagues, and arriving punctu-
ally so that our time together is most effectively and efficiently
spent. We have a highly important issue to discuss today . . . you will
recall that eight months ago we identified and charged a panel of

administrators, teachers, parents, community business representatives, and three students to explore our mathematics curriculum and its program outcomes for our students. After four months of diligent study, this committee recommended the adoption of a new approach to teaching and learning mathematics that would result in students' engagement in increased critical thinking and problem solving."

"Yes, this curriculum," Jan Bradson agreed, "the committee believes, will serve to provide opportunities for students gaining expertise in new knowledge and skills in alignment with expectations for what are deemed the futuristic needs of our students. I served on the committee, and to that end, we adopted, with great fanfare, The Great Mathematics curriculum for all grades, K through seniors in high school."

"Indeed, four months ago," Superintendent McElroy continued, "the curriculum materials and required resources were obtained and distributed to all the schools, personnel and policy adjustments were made, and three consultants spent a week with us immediately prior to our schools' fall opening. But, as you and I have done our 'walk throughs' of the schools along with the principals and teacher leaders, we are in agreement that we are seeing nearly nothing to suggest that the new program and its instructional practices are being given attention by more than a very few classroom teachers in the middle and high schools. I even saw, in one classroom, the instructional guide to this curriculum holding up a flower pot on the bookshelf!"

"Ho, that would be laughable, if not so distressing," noted Will Saunders. "What is the problem here?"

At this point, Victoria Lopez offered a possibility. "Albert Vermillion and I just finished a short course at the university last month. That course focused on school change and improvement. A consistent theme that persisted throughout the course of how to improve schools was this idea:

> *Improvement in any organization* is based on *changing* elements that are not working productively for elements that have the potential to work more effectively, and this *change* is based on *learning*—what the change is and how to use it.

We know what the name of our change is—that is, the new mathematics curriculum, The Great Mathematics—but do we know what the new curriculum comprises and how to make it work with our students?"

To this, McElroy responded, "You raise a very good point, Victoria. As you all have been looking into the introduction and implementation of the new math, you have shared your notes of your observations, your questions, and your concerns. And, although we are just four months into this change of curriculum and its practices and don't expect great progress, we ought to be seeing some efforts to use it. Over all, that is not happening."

"However, interesting reports have come from the observations of two schools. It seems that in these schools, the principal and/or the teacher leaders have come together and have acquired additional help in learning about and understanding the new curriculum and engaging teachers in deep learning about the what and how of this new approach, and subsequently, using the new practices with students in classrooms. Clearly, we have ignored the significant role of the schools' leadership in contributing to this effort."

CHANGE MAKERS—CHANGE LEADERS

Albert Vermillion chimed in, "Vicki and I, in our coursework, studied some of the writing by Peter Block on leadership and community. We found what I think is a very useful definition of leadership:

Leadership is the process of translating intention into reality.

"This pithy definition helps us to understand that leadership is not necessarily a single leader but multiple individuals collectively exercising leadership skills. These skills enable a group to collectively articulate a goal for enhancement or improvement, whether it is a school, a church choir, a football team, the guys in the produce section of the grocery store, or so on. The goal articulation, supported by leadership, identifies a new element or means for improving the organization's status, and, in addition, leadership provides the wherewithal to reach that goal. Creating a mental image of the results of the goal aids in moving toward achievement of the goal."

"So," Charlie Yin concluded, "we could also say that many of us have been 'change seekers,' especially all who have been involved in the study and determination of the new math program. We could go beyond that and suggest that each of us on the entire district and campus staffs should always be looking for new ways of teaching and learning so that we are consistently learning about more effective instructional strategies and for creating an environment conducive to changing practices (such as Karen Seashore Louis has described in the previous chapter). Our profession, the press, and our public expect no less of us. And today it appears we have an immediate situation to address."

"Thanks to all of you for your contributions," McElroy replied. "It appears that we are all on the same page and have an initial understanding of our situation. One thing that is quite clear, and I invite your comments, is that our leaders in our schools—principals and teacher-leaders—require learning more about the role that they should be playing. This should happen now, in order to help them to learn what that role should be in supporting the implementation of the new curriculum, supporting the teaching staff in learning about their roles and work with the new mathematics program. We must pursue this now . . . so, we will meet at the end of this week on Friday afternoon at 3:00 p.m. and adjourn at 6:00 in order to reorganize and attend the Friday night football game."

WHO ARE CHANGE LEADERS?

Anyone in any role who is responsible for change and improvement occurring successfully in the organization is a leader of change. At the school campus level, this could be the principal, assistant principal, teacher department chairs in middle and high schools, grade-level chairs in elementary schools, coaches, or instructional guides, to name the most likely. We know from the school change research that someone must guide—providing support and appropriate pressure—the educators who are adopting and implementing new practices that have the potential or promise to translate into desired outcomes for students.

The ultimate beneficiaries are students, but before student outcomes can be realized, the adult educators must learn identified new practices related to the desired student outcomes and transfer their new learning and practices to classrooms (see Figure 2.1).

Figure 2.1   Relationship Between Professional Learning and Student Results

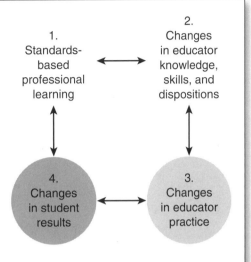

1. When professional learning is standards-based, it has greater potential to change what educators know, are able to do, and believe.

2. When educators' knowledge, skills, and dispositions change, they have a broader repertoire of effective strategies to use to adapt their practices to meet performance expectations and student learning needs.

3. When educator practice improves, students have a greater likelihood of achieving results.

4. When student results improve, the cycle repeats for continuous improvement.

This cycle works two ways: If educators are not achieving the results they want, they determine what changes in practice are needed and then what knowledge, skills, and dispositions are needed to make the desired changes. They then consider how to apply the standards so that they can engage in the learning needed to strengthen their practice.

Source: Learning Forward. *Standards for Professional Learning*, 2011. ©Learning Forward.

This figure illustrates the sequence of the adult-educators' professional learning (Steps 1, 2, 3) and the subsequent student learning outcomes or results (Step 4). There is a myth, rampant across the education landscape and beyond, that suggests professional learning impacts students directly. This is not the case—never. Professional learning is directed to precisely what it says—to the professionals, teachers, and administrators. They are the first learners, and, as such, require support and assistance in their learning. Their learning is supported by change leaders. Thus, change leaders' essential role of support in improving teaching and learning in the school and across the district must be developed. And what exactly is this role?

THE ROLE OF LEADERS FOR PROFESSIONAL LEARNING AND CHANGE

In its articulation of the revised Standards for Professional Learning (Learning Forward, 2011), Learning Forward was clear to convey the leadership necessary for professional learning, change, and improvement. Three major components of this leadership activity were identified (Learning Forward, 2011, pp. 28–30):

- Develop capacity for learning and leading
- Advocate for professional learning
- Create support systems and structures

These three big ideas of the leadership standard were further defined through construction of a series of Innovation Configuration (IC) Maps that articulated specific actions of leaders at the school level. While the following items come from the IC Maps for the principal (Learning Forward, 2012, pp. 201–211), highly similar maps have been created for coaches and the school leadership team (see Learning Forward, 2012, for these materials):

- Develop capacity for learning and leading

  o Commits to continuous professional learning
  o Develops own and others' capacity for leadership of professional learning
  o Understands and uses the Standards for Professional Learning in making decisions about professional learning
  o Serves as a leader of professional learning
  o Coaches and supervises school-based facilitators of professional learning

- Advocate for professional learning

  o Articulates the link between student learning and professional learning
  o Advocates high-quality professional learning

- Create support systems and structures

  o Establishes systems and structures for effective professional learning
  o Prepares and supports staff for skillful collaboration

o Cultivates and maintains a collaborative culture
o Creates expectations for collaborative professional learning within the school day

Similar IC maps framed by these same three big ideas of leadership, at the system level, were created for central office, director of professional learning, superintendent, and school board (Learning Forward, 2013).

Remember that the standards do not function in isolation from one another. The first standard, that of learning communities, is a rich source from which school-based and system-level leaders can become firmly grounded in the cycle of continuous improvement. This cycle is an essential tool for leadership teams' use in planning and conducting professional learning for school change and improvement at the system and school levels. This cycle may be found, explicated in rich detail, in the Learning Communities volume of this series of seven books, each of which is devoted to one of the seven standards (Chapter 2: Hord & Roy, pp. 19–60, in Lieberman, Miller, Hord, Roy, & von Frank, 2014).

This discussion of the leadership standard, thus far, has provided information about who may be involved as leaders for promoting and supporting professional learning at the school or district level. It has also focused attention on the actions or behaviors expected of such leaders. But, if such leadership does not exist at a particular site, how can it be developed and implemented?

CHANGING LARVAE INTO BUTTERFLIES

The metamorphosis of egg into mature butterfly is a complex one that requires four stages of growth and development. These must occur before the mature, magnificent creature breaks its confining chrysalis and emerges with wings moving to dry body moisture and fly into its new universe. The learning, growth, and development of individuals moving into leadership roles is no less challenging, particularly for developing the collaborative leadership now demanded of today's schools and districts.

Research on the change process in schools (Hall & Hord, 2015) is consistent with the research on professional development for educators (Joyce & Calhoun, 2010). These two bodies of work are clear in their findings about adults' learning needs. This section of the chapter is devoted to the strategies or steps required to enable individuals to change their knowledge and skills, behaviors, and dispositions in order to assume and implement the new roles and their required practices as leaders of professional learning and change. There are six strategies from the change research; the professional development research fits prominently into the third strategy for investing in professional learning.

Articulating a Shared Vision of the Change

Most everyone would agree that it is impossible to reach a desired outcome or result unless a picture, or mental image, has been created to clearly identify and describe this end point. This is true whether one is planning a holiday trip, embarking on losing weight, using an electronic communications tool of advanced complexity, or such.

The desired end point of the district administrative team that introduced this chapter is that of leadership at the school and district levels that will

- advocate for continuous professional learning;
- develop the capacity for learning and leading for themselves and their staffs;
- provide support structures and systems for professional learning;
- develop and enact the role of supporting and pushing/persuading school personnel to adopt, learn, and implement new classroom practices; and to
- become continuous learners and leaders of change with their staffs.

Fortunately, we have a clear picture of this leadership and its desired behaviors provided by Learning Forward and formatted in the IC maps to which we referred earlier in this chapter. The IC maps and several additional references provide ever-increasing clarity and complexity to what this leadership should look like and be doing related to the leadership standard. A listing of such references is noted at the end of this chapter, but remember to give attention to the leadership role in the learning organization, described by Karen Seashore in Chapter 1 of this volume.

Essentially, clarity about what effective leadership will look like in our schools and districts where it is supporting and promoting the professional learning of the staff is an imperative. Whether an existing IC map is used or one is created to represent the ideal that is desired in any specific locale (Hord & Roussin, 2013), this tool is an excellent one for communicating the vision. Applications of the IC map can be used in additional strategies required for the process of implementing the leadership standard and will be noted in the strategies that follow.

The first strategy for implementing the leadership standard has been introduced. The IC Map has been encouraged as a tool for clarifying and communicating the vision of such leadership. What are the subsequent strategies in which to engage for achieving successful leadership implementation?

Creating a Plan for Implementing the New Vision

This plan should focus on activities that will ensure the creation of the content knowledge base and the skills demanded of the leaders involved in the new vision for leadership. It should accommodate the needs and concerns of these potential leaders who are the focus of attention. The plan will also make it possible to identify the resources required for putting the planning document's activities into operation. And what might these considerations be?

Budgets will surely play a prime role in adopting and implementing new roles for the school and district leadership. The leadership standard recommends three major roles for these individuals; fulfilling these roles and the time and attention required may seriously impact these school staff members' time and the resulting need for additional staff or the realignment of existing staff. Material and human resources (such as consultants and coaches for the learners) will undoubtedly be necessary if the learning process of the leaders is to be successful. Various policy changes may dictate additional needs for budget consideration.

A major issue for attention is the time required for the learning leaders to gain the expertise expected. Across the United States, we typically demonstrate impatience for productivity; we want success right now. Understanding the time and resources required for this learning process, that will be addressed in the next strategy, is of the utmost importance. "Push and support" is suggested as two approaches to the frequently struggling learners of new roles. Without a measure of patience (with persistence) from the individuals conducting the change for the leadership role, frustration, increased stress, and lack of trust in the learning-to-be-new-leaders process will land on the garbage heap of failed innovations in school change and improvement.

This suggests the understanding that, while a plan should be based on thoughtful action and desired outcomes, the original plan is not cast in concrete. Changing conditions and unexpected happenings may easily create the need for rethinking and adjusting the plan. On the other hand, changing the plan with great frequency may result in frustration for the learners . . . keeping one's eye on the outcomes and a finger on the pulse of the participant learners as well as on district conditions are tactics of the wise change facilitator.

The plan must drive thoughtfully, clearly, and forcefully to the results specified in the vision. This is its purpose; therefore, it is to be used to guide the learning and implementation of the vision, which directs our attention to the learning strategy.

Investing in Professional Learning of the Vision

It was stated earlier, and it bears repeating

Improvement is based on *change* and change requires *learning* what the change is and how to use it.

This explicit connection between change and learning provides a basic reason for the standards for professional learning. The learning that grounds and expands the knowledge and skills of educational professionals must be of the highest quality so that the continuous learning of the professionals is, in a word, powerful—for the adult learning is the predecessor to student learning.

Keep in mind that the learning and transformation of school and district personnel into change leaders will happen on two levels: on the first level, in our story that initiated this chapter, the superintendent and district staff will learn what change leaders do (see *The Role of Leaders for Professional Learning and Change* on page 42) and how they operate in this role. The district administrators will serve as colearners about this role with principals (the second level) in the schools. When it is possible to break the barriers between district office and principals in the schools and engage them in collegial learning, collaboration can be strengthened. These colearners employ their new knowledge and behaviors as change leaders to teach and tutor others—a third level, teacher leaders in the schools—to become change leaders/facilitators and support teachers who are implementing new practice.

This is a high-level change in roles for these administrators, and significant time and resources should be brought to its successful end.

Far too often, educators have been given a short paper that gives direction for new roles. Far too often, educators are given a two-hour lecture about what a new role looks like. Neither of these approaches will produce the knowledge and skills necessary for successful change leadership. We turn to research on professional development/ professional learning for guidance.

Beginning in the late eighties, Bruce Joyce and Beverly Showers began investigating, through robust research methods and approaches, how professional learning has been conducted and the results of its endeavors. From the findings of their observations, data collection, and analyses, they identified four components (numbered below) that were offered for the learning of adults and their effects on the adult learners—the following list includes the percentage of participants' attainment of the outcomes, Knowledge Attainment, Skills Development, and Transfer/Implementation:

1. Adult learners who read about or were lectured about a new practice (program or process) achieved 10 percent Knowledge, 5 percent Skill, and no Transfer/Implementation of the new practice into their classrooms.

2. Adding demonstrations or modeling of the new practice resulted in 30 percent Knowledge, 20 percent Skill, and no gains for Transfer or Implementation.

3. Learners practicing the "new way" accompanied by feedback produced increases to 60 percent in Knowledge and Skills but only 5 percent success in Transfer/Implementation into the classroom.

4. A significant increase in all results—95 percent—of Knowledge, Skills, and Transfer/Implementation occurred with the cumulative use of the first three components and the addition of peer coaching.

Changing classroom and school practice requires that adult educators learn what the change is and how to apply it. The attention of coaches, revealed in this research, is clearly important to support adults' learning process. Subsequent research findings from the work of Joyce and Calhoun (2010) reinforce the significance of coaches' involvement in both short-term and long-term use of new practice:

> When reading, discussion, and lectures about the new practice were employed, the effects on participants' knowledge was "very positive." The effects on short-term as well as long-term use was 5 percent to 10 percent.
>
> The three study activities (reading, discussion, lectures) and the addition of multiple demonstrations effected knowledge very positively. Short-term use was achieved by 5 percent to 20 percent of the participants, and long-term use scored 5 percent to 10 percent.
>
> The study, demonstrations, and participants' planning units and lessons resulted in very positive effects on knowledge, 80 percent to 90 percent on short-term use and 5 percent 10 percent long-term use.
>
> Finally, employing all three of the components (study, demonstrations, planning units and lessons) plus coaching resulted in very positive effects on knowledge, 90-plus percent on participants' short-term use and 90-plus percent on long-term use.

It is clear that significant value is produced through the engagement of coaches with the learners. These findings about coaches and the now widespread use of coaches in supporting principals and teachers in their mastery of learning about new practices, processes, roles, and so on, demands their provision. The power of using coaches to support adult learning poses another challenge—providing these facilitating coaches. It becomes another task for the change leaders, whether these leaders reside in the district office or at the campus-based school.

It is clear that substantial human and other resources, such as time, are required for the successful learning of our educators and that change leaders at the district and school levels must give attention to the provision of these resources. Much has been noted about the role of coaches and the importance they have for the learning and support of the leaders and the implementers of any change.

A last word about this strategy . . .

See the volume on the standard for learning designs for further information (Drago-Severson, Roy, & von Frank, 2015) about components and processes that deliver significant results for adult learning.

Assessing Progress

There are many would-be change leaders/facilitators who assume that when participants in a change effort attend a two- or three-day workshop, they have had sufficient attention and activities to understand well what the envisioned change is and how it will work. Most unfortunately, this assumption is far from reality. These beginning sentences suggest that conducting a workshop for a few days will NOT do it—whatever *it* is.

As the learning components of the research models in the previous section reveal, learning is a complex, long-term endeavor, and the more complex the change is, the longer and more support for individuals will be required. The factor that was revealed as very influential in the adults' learning was coaching (Joyce & Calhoun, 2010; Joyce & Showers, 2002). Coaching is the foundation of monitoring progress. As an aside, a more agreeable term for this action might be *observing* progress that does not carry the negative connotation frequently associated with monitoring or assessing progress. Often, the monitoring or observing is an emotionally charged activity, for both the change leader/facilitator and the individual who is learning about the change and how to implement and use it.

Note the word, *individual*. The most effective monitoring is done one person at a time. Most certainly, individuals work in groups at times and might be observed while doing so. Observation of the implementer in action with some guiding protocol for the observation (i.e., IC map) is probably the most potent means of monitoring. A second useful means for gaining information about the implementer's successful learning and his or her implementation of it in the classroom (or wherever the intended site) is the interaction gained from a collegial conversation in a quiet, nondisturbable location, where both the facilitator and the implementer can be comfortable.

Putting the implementing individual across a table from the change leader/facilitator makes many implementers who are challenged by the learning of new instructional strategies, or whatever the innovation, anxious. The sensitive leader will arrange to seat the implementer and himself or herself side by side, so as to be on equal terms. This also allows the two to review the protocol collegially, encouraging commentary from both individuals.

Many change leaders are initially shy in this observation, or collegial checking and facilitating, role. The implementing teacher may also be initially uncomfortable in the observation or conversation about his or her classroom work. Despite these feelings in either party, and to dispel them, the leader takes the first action, and it should be one of welcoming, warmth, and acceptance. The implementer is encouraged to solicit help or assistance, but if this does not happen, the leader conducts additional "let's get on the same page" visits. The charge is to establish a positive working relationship, based on mutual respect and regard.

This also means that the leader keeps relevant notes about each implementer that she or he is supporting in order to maintain familiarity with the implementer's challenges, successes, and needs for support. And, of course, the leader will always check back to ascertain whether the support that was provided was useful. One tool that can be used to guide support and to note its success is the IC map. This tool was introduced in the first strategy/activity of the change leader's efforts. The IC map indicates *what the implementer should be doing* and is used to compare to *what the implementer is doing*. The resulting gap between these two constitutes the basis for the change leader's provision of support, the focus of attention in the next strategy. Change leaders can guide the school's group of implementing teachers in constructing such a map (Hord & Roussin, 2013). This map communicates what should be happening by the implementer, providing a guide for him or her and the leader in developing the implementer's expertise with the change/innovation.

You will find a similar discussion of these findings focused on the six strategies essential for implementing new policies, practices, and roles in the implementation volume of this series of books directed to the standards (Fullan, Hord, & von Frank, 2015, Chapter 2).

Providing Assistance and Support

In the previous section, a strong pitch was made for monitoring and assessing the progress that the adult learners, the implementers of the new practice, are making. The challenge is to invest much attention to each implementer, to know at what point each has reached in his or her learning about the innovation and how to put it into practice in his or her classroom or in the principals' domain. When the change leaders have collected these data, the end point has not been reached, as most implementers will require substantial support for a great deal of time. This is a challenging and significant action of coaches/facilitators and requires abundant time and resourcefulness in order to effectively aid implementers' success.

Now is the time to study the data that were collected and to plan thoughtful and appropriate assistance and support. Assessing (the previous strategy discussed above) and assisting are like the proverbial hand in glove, suggesting a very strong relationship between these two strategies that the change leaders will undertake.

Data acquired from use of the IC map will help the leader to ascertain where on the chart the implementer has progressed: Is this individual rated toward the right side of the horizontal continuum, indicating that this implementer has not progressed very far in his or her learning and implementing the new practice? This would not be an unusual circumstance for early users. Several who are much alike in their current progress might be joined in a group of three to four for a small group intervention, a supportive action to help them understand better what the innovation/change leader role is and how to install it in their schools for effective use with staff and others. Differentiation is the key word here. Some implementers will require close and consistent individual attention and support.

On the other hand, as the adults' innovation learning advances and they are making consistent progress, there will be some who can be judged to support others—their peers. Developing the skills of these who show the promise of early understanding and use of the innovation contributes to the creation of a larger pool of "learning leaders" or "leaders of learning" who can support others as well as continue to refine their own innovation use.

This is a time to make certain that trust abounds—of leaders and implementers and implementers with other implementers, of district administrators and school-based principals. Certainly, trust should be given continuous attention, unceasing time, and with specific activities for developing it. It should be a part of the district and school's culture, an important aspect of the potential leader's change readiness and his or her acceptance of risk taking. Aspects of this trust could include the following (Tschannen-Moran, 2004):

Honesty—truth telling; honoring promises and agreements

Openness—conducting open conversation; sharing information, decision making, and power; delegating

Reliability—demonstrating dependability and consistency, commitment and diligence

Competence—setting standards and examples and pushing for results; resolving rather than avoiding conflict; demonstrating flexibility

Benevolence—supporting others and extending goodwill, caring and expressing appreciation for efforts

These elements, embedded in the members of an organization, represent positive and supportive characteristics of a collaborative culture. The organization's leadership exhibits these characteristics and also takes action to develop these characteristics in its members. Trusting and trustworthy members work successfully together to ensure increased effectiveness of the organization. Thus, not only the leaders but all individuals in the organization share these characteristics. The leaders will work continuously to develop and establish and maintain a high level of trust across the group.

In addition to the ongoing attention to building and maintaining trust, there are actions that can be provided to the implementers. The data collected about an implementer's progress will dictate the kind of support needed by the individual.

A generalized list of suggestions for consideration of supporting implementers with ongoing assistance may be found in *Taking Charge of Change* (Hord, Rutherford, Huling, & Hall, 2014). These interventions (p. 75) related to providing ongoing assistance to support implementers include the following:

Ongoing Assistance
- Providing feedback on the use of the innovation
- Providing ongoing, on-time coaching
- Providing personalized technical assistance
- Creating additional opportunities for collaborative professional learning related to the innovation
- Celebrating successes
- Clarifying innovation misconceptions
- Conferencing with implementers about implementation and impact data

It should not be surprising that these assisting actions can be used productively and appropriately with other stages or strategies of the series. Creating the assistance and support at all stages should be thoughtful, meaningful, based on data that have been collected, and appropriate for the particular individual. A second tool that can be used easily to gain data/information about implementers is stages of concern (see Hord & Roussin, 2013).

A major consideration, already noted, is the creation of a warm, accepting, and mutually respectful relationship that supports the assessment (strategy four) and the facilitator's response to the data (strategy five). Because the provision of assistance is highly dependent on the progress of the individual, it is challenging to expand a never-ending list of appropriate responses for a single individual. This activity should, however, be the *modus operandi* of the leader who keeps a journal of successful assistance, possibilities that respond to various data-revealed needs of implementers. Frequent meetings and interactions with other leaders who are facilitating the adult learning and its transfer into the work site can be a rich source of supporting responses and actions provided by the leader. The leader is a continuous learner, always searching for new, useful, and realistic suggestions to provide the continuing assistance required of the implementers. The collaborative and trusting environment, noted previously, adds significantly to the assessing-assisting strategies discussed here. But a few words directed to such an environment are considered next.

Creating a Context That Supports Change

Through trial and error in using new practices, many educators find a way that works to their satisfaction; they become comfortable and routinely conduct learning activities related to the new practice with little to no variation (some will think of Levels of Use here; if so, see Hord & Roussin, 2013). These individuals have ironed out the wrinkles of curriculum and other programs and processes so that they work "okay" for them in their classrooms. To disrupt this stable and comfortable condition can be very threatening and anxiety producing to school and district staff members.

However, this complacent school, if it is not serving its students so that they achieve expected outcomes, will require disruption. In this complacent school setting, as in any school, the context strongly impacts the staff and does so through two components: one is the *physical features*, such as facilities, the building (its condition and appeal, space for playgrounds and a significant library, adequate and appropriate furnishings for the ages and sizes of students), and organizational structures such as schedules and policies. In one poorly performing high school, as part of a research study, students were given the privilege and responsibility of painting the entry floor walls and with designing and painting floor-to-ceiling-size colorful murals. Not only did this enliven a dreadfully drab physical environment, but the students could claim it as their school that they renovated themselves. It influenced the staff as well. A serious sense of pride developed that moved into classrooms and appeared to activate teachers to higher energy and to motivate students to give greater attention to teaching and learning. The result was a context where staff and students changed to more productive behaviors.

The second component is the *human element*, comprising, obviously, the organization's inhabitants, their values and beliefs, and the norms that appear to influence their attitudes, behaviors, and relationships. These two components interact and impact each other. The presence or absence of trust is another factor that significantly contributes to encouraging a staff members' positive involvement in a change. The creation and enhancement of trust throughout any change effort is to be largely encouraged.

The use of Stages of Concern (SoC) can be helpful in obtaining a sense of how the individual staff member is reacting or responding to a change and its implementation. SoC data can be collected in three ways: through a rather formal 35-item questionnaire, through asking participants to write several sentences or a brief paragraph about their concerns, or by conducting a "one-legged" conference, that is a three- to four-minute informal but structured conversation with an individual to gain understanding of his or her concerns—attitudes, reactions, the affective dimension (see Hord & Roussin, 2013 for how to conduct these data collections).

The goal is to create a context in which leaders, teachers, students, and parents value change as a means to increase the effectiveness of teaching and learning. In this context, all consistently seek new ideas, practices, and processes and collaboratively work to include promising changes in the school. In this way, everyone becomes a change seeker and contributes to a culture of continuous improvement, based on change.

In this context (reported by Hord et al., 2014), school leaders work to create the underlying culture by

- managing schedules and structures so that people can come together to share ideas for improvement, and they allocate resources to support improvement efforts;
- developing policies for increasing staff capacity;
- modeling the behaviors that they hope the staff will adopt through being highly visible to the staff and working collaboratively with them, exhibiting focus and commitment;
- serving as teachers and coaches for the staff, through reading, studying, and sharing materials that contribute to the staff members' developing expertise and attending professional learning activities with the staff;
- engaging in conflict resolution and using it with the staff members as a means to resolve disputes and build unity; and
- using the selection and termination processes to ensure that staff commit to school goals, recognizing staff's work publicly and privately, as well as inviting staff to share their efforts and experiences as they drive toward goal attainment (p. 82).

This identification of activities provides guidance to the change leaders and clearly suggests the comprehensiveness and complexity of activities useful for adopting and implementing change. It also clearly illustrates the need for multiple leaders to do this extensive work, thus a change leadership team.

Serving as a school leader, which by definition is leading and guiding change (see Peter Block's quotation), includes a large-scale set of tasks. However, there are, in addition to the six strategies discussed here, two other sets of expectations of leaders.

ALIGNMENT OF STANDARDS, IMPLEMENTATION STRATEGIES, AND CYCLE OF CONTINUOUS IMPROVEMENT

One could state, with a large degree of certainty, that all districts across the universe are expected to engage annually in school/district performance review and to create improvement plans for the upcoming year(s). Involvement in very small and remote districts may be limited to the superintendent, while in very large districts there could be involvement by representatives from the schools and central offices, the community of parents and possibly of business, and, in a few cases, of students and perhaps a consultant or two to support the process. In any case, almost always the process for doing so includes the following steps taken as an example from Learning Forward's Cycle of Continuous Improvement (Learning Forward, 2011, p. 24), for which school change leaders must be aware and prepared:

1. Use data to determine area(s) of students' low performance.

2. Use data to identify teacher and system variables that contribute to or diminish the quality of teaching and learning.

3. Construct student learning goals that address poor performance.

4. Identify educator learning goals that relate to student goals.

5. Explore and select evidence-based knowledge and skills for educators' learning to address students' goals.

6. Implement/transfer the educators' learning through support and coaching.

7. Use monitoring activities to assess and refine implementation/transfer.

8. Celebrate results and evaluate.

These steps have been simplified a bit for easier understanding. Nonetheless, a set of steps for the cycle of continuous improvement, the seven standards for professional learning, and the six strategies required for implementing new practices constitute major tasks for leaders. But these three sets appear remarkably parallel and in alignment with one another (see Figure 2.2).

Review the column of research-based strategies that have comprised the major text of this chapter. Then compare the strategies with the standards column.

The three standards (learning communities, leadership, resources) represent the factors that contribute to the specific context in which the leader/leadership team operates. Then study each horizontal section of the chart to ascertain how the strategies, the standards, and the steps of the cycle of continuous improvement share related knowledge, skills, and dispositions—yet each individual unit has substantive differences that can enhance the understanding of leaders for their professional learning and change and how they will conduct the learning for change and improvement projects with appropriate school or district staff members.

Figure 2.2 Alignment of Strategies, Standards, and the Cycle of Continuous Improvement

	Research-Based Strategies	LF Standards for Prof. Learning	Cycle of Continuous Improvement
Contextual Factors in Place	Create a context conducive to change	Learning communities	
		Leadership	
		Resources	
Analysis and Decisions		Data	Identify student and (related) educator learning needs
	Clarify vision (results/ outcomes)	Outcomes	Articulate student outcomes and related educator learning goals
			Select new practices/ program to achieve educator and student results
Implementation of Educator Learning, Transfer to Student Sites	Plan implementation		
	Conduct professional learning	Learning designs	Provide adult learning sessions and follow-up coaching to achieve educator goals
	Monitor educator use of new practices	Implementation	Transfer educator learning to work site with support
	Provide continuous support and assistance	Outcomes	Transfer educator learning to work site with support

The chart is an endeavor to simplify and streamline leaders' study and preparation for adopting the actions of the three models contained in the chart. The chart suggests the relationships of three sets of challenging actions expected of leaders as they address professional learning, change, and improvement.

In addition to these somewhat global entities, there are constructs and tools to assess/diagnose where *each* individual is in the process of learning about, adopting, and implementing a change. Such assessments make it possible to provide differentiated/individualized support and assistance at every stage or step of the change/improvement effort. Leaders will find these tools very reliable for collecting data and, subsequently, useful in the determination of each individual's needs as he or she progresses through the challenges of implementation. These change process tools are as follows:

- IC maps were given substantial attention in the strategies discussed above. The use of the maps is especially valuable for identifying what the change is and what the implementers are expected to be doing relative to it. Its chart format makes it possible to mark and record where implementers are succeeding or struggling in their implementation efforts.
- SoC, earlier mentioned modestly, enlightens the leaders of change about implementers' attitudes, reactions, and feelings about the change and their role in its implementation.
- Levels of Use (LoU) is a third tool that reveals information about the individual. In this case, rather than feelings (the affective factors), LoU provides the leader with data on which to draw insights into the approach or behaviors that the implementer is expressing or exhibiting. Because these behaviors are observable, many leaders find LoU more valuable in their work of supporting the changers.
- Descriptive information about these constructs and their associated tools/methods for measuring the individual's progress with each construct may be found in Hall and Hord (2015). This reference explains the *what* of the constructs and their tools. However, these constructs and their tools are also the topic of attention in a second text. This text is organized as small lessons to direct and support leaders to understand and be guided in *how* to use the material. This may be found in Hord and Roussin (2013).

As a result of reviewing the expectations of leaders noted in the chart, it would not be difficult to assert that the roles of leaders who promote professional learning, change, and improvement are many and vitally important to an effective school. Such a school is one in which all students are served well, according to their individual needs and learning capacities. The leaders in their schools and districts have a great deal on their agendas.

LOOSELY OR TIGHTLY COUPLED: DOES IT MATTER?

Considering the expansive role that school leaders are expected to play, the question that is immediately asked is, Who is responsible for the professional learning of the leaders, and how do they do it? These leaders are expected to develop capacity for learning and leading, to advocate for professional learning, and to create support systems and structures for accomplishing it all. Principals in the schools, a primary target for this book, are expected to not only learn about and express these activities but also to develop these components in additional potential leaders.

For the first part of these expectations, that is the development of the school-based primary leader, the principal; the superintendent and his cabinet in the scenario that opened this chapter are investigating what can be done to develop their principals. Learning Forward has defined the three major roles of the school-based leader (see paragraph above). Marzano and Waters (2009) maintain that district leaders that are tightly coupled with their school-based leaders can effectively impact activities in the schools and achievement results of students—the ultimate outcome that drives the work of districts and schools. Tightly coupled means that the district leadership

ensures collaborative goal setting,

establishes non-negotiable goals for achievement and instruction,

creates the board's alignment with and support of the district's goals, monitors the goals, and

allocates resources to support the goals (Marzano & Waters, 2009, p. 22).

Could it be that Superintendent Homero McElroy is on the way to tight coupling with professional learning for principals and increased achievement for students?

On the other hand, McElroy and his cabinet may consider a more loosely coupled model of district and school-based leadership. Ash and D'Auria (2013) write about *School Systems That Learn*, where across the pages runs the continuous theme of developing capacity at all levels and across all role groups. They promote relationship elements in their suggestions for how district office and school-based leaders might interact productively. They cite four drivers that support and encourage learning and its application by principals and teachers for improving outcomes for students:

1. Importance of trust—Characteristics of trust and trustworthiness are exemplified by individuals' respect and regard for others and for the competence that each demonstrates. Each individual is recognized for the particular competencies he or she has, not expected to be expert in all competencies. Thus, the individual is valued for the unique skills and knowledge that she or he contributes to the work of the group. In addition, following up to take action on promises made demonstrates integrity, another element that builds trust; failure to act diminishes the trust.

2. Boundless collaboration—This interdependent interaction occurs vertically up and down the system (think here the superintendent's team and the schools' principals) or across the system horizontally, taking in those at the same or similar position (think principals and assistant principals at all schools in the district). Collaboration is seen intra- and inter-school (*intra* meaning within the school; *inter* means across the schools). Collaboration is seen as a powerful factor to support staff members' learning and growth and in problem solving with the system's collaborating inhabitants. (Ash & D'Auria, 2013, p. 78)

3. Capacity building—The district pays particular attention to building the capacity of the principals (look back at the story of the superintendent's cabinet meeting) and of all staff. The belief is that principals' and teachers' professional learning

will be directed toward and supportive of students' needs, teaching quality will increase for their students, and students will gain. This sequence reveals another aspect of the leaders' role in supporting the staff members' learning and explains the indirect but significant link between effective professional learning and student performance.

4. Leadership at all levels—The authors identify attributes required of leaders who work with others "to educate all students to high levels." These attributes are to act on their core values, inspire confidence, build an inclusive network, build a positive school culture, demonstrate sincere inquiry, and support risk taking. (Ash & D'Auria, 2013, p. 13)

Whether any district or campus leader determines to use a tightly or loosely coupled approach for working to bring about staff members' professional learning about a change and its implementation so that it benefits students may well be based on the leader's beliefs, experiences, and preferred style of leading or on the established culture of the school or district. It behooves any leader to examine the context and its defining characteristics and to select the most compelling approach to providing professional learning for the staff so that change and improvement are successful.

CONCLUSION

This chapter's focus has been on implementing the leader's role in his or her everyday practice (expectations identified by Learning Forward, 2011):

Developing staff's capacity for learning and leading

Advocating for professional learning

Creating support systems and structures for the first two

A secondary focus was on school leaders' school change and improvement efforts, based on their provision of high-quality professional learning. The research-based strategies and techniques for implementing new roles are those used for implementing any new practice, program, or process, such as a curriculum program or a new process for student discipline. The strategies for implementation remain the same, with some possible tweaks or adjustments for any specific innovation. Fortunately, rigorous research-based strategies and tools have been created, field tested and used by many school and district leaders globally. Gaining expertise in integrating the information and insights reported in this modest chapter requires courage, commitment, and the will and stamina to stay the course. The availability of facilitators, coaches, or colleagues experienced in the role of coaches can be exceptionally helpful and valued.

"Improvement is a continuous process without beginning or end. Because professional learning is at the core of every effort to increase educator effectiveness and results for all students, its quality and effectiveness cannot be left to chance" (Learning Forward, 2011, p. 55). Research has informed us multiple times (see Seashore, Chapter 1 of this volume) about the productive power that school leaders can draw on to support a school staff's attention and activities to learning and its transition to the classroom where it benefits students.

This chapter is dedicated to those leaders, continuously learning themselves, seeking change and providing for the effective learning of the professionals in the school where all are learning together so that all lead together, for our students. And please refer to the chapter's introductory quotation and note that our educational leaders are

stretching out to mend the part of the world that is within reach.

Readings of the Leadership Standard, published by Learning Forward, include the following:

Crow, T. (2012, December). From the editor, leadership, *JSD, 33*(6), 4.

Hirsh, S., & Hord, S. (2012). *A playbook for professional learning: Putting the standards into action* (Chapter 2). Oxford, OH: Learning Forward.

Learning Forward. (2011). *Standards for professional learning* (pp. 28–30). Oxford, OH: Author

Learning Forward. (2012). *Standards into practice: School-based roles. Innovation configuration maps for standards for professional learning.* Oxford, OH: Author.

Learning Forward. (2013). *Standards into practice: School system roles. Innovation configuration maps for standards for professional learning.* Oxford, OH: Author.

Wahlstrom, K. L., & York-Barr, J. (2011, August). Leadership support and structures make the difference for educators and students. *JSD, 32*(4).

REFERENCES

Ash, P. B., & D'Auria, J. (2013). *School systems that learn: Improving professional practice, overcoming limitations, and diffusing innovation.* Thousand Oaks, CA: Corwin.

Drago-Severson, E., Roy, P., & von Frank, V. (2015). *Reach the highest standard in professional learning: Learning designs.* Thousand Oaks, CA: Corwin & Learning Forward.

Fullan, M., Hord, S. M, & von Frank, V. (2015). *Reach the highest standard in professional learning: Implementation.* Thousand Oaks, CA: Corwin & Learning Forward.

Hall, G. E., & Hord, S. M. (2015). *Implementing change: Patterns, principles, and potholes* (4th Ed.). Boston, MA: Pearson.

Hord, S. M., & Roussin, J. L. (2013). *Implementing change through learning: Concerns-based concepts tools, and strategies for guiding change.* Thousand Oaks, CA: Corwin.

Hord, S. M, Rutherford, W. L., Huling, L., & Hall, G. E. (2014). *Taking charge of change.* Austin, TX: SEDL.

Joyce, B., & Calhoun, E. (2010). *Models of professional development: A celebration of educators.* Thousand Oaks, CA: Corwin & NSDC.

Joyce, B., & Showers, B. (2002). *Student achievement through staff development* (3rd ed.). Alexandria, VA: Association for Supervision and Curriculum Development.

Learning Forward. (2011). *Standards for professional learning.* Oxford, OH: Author.

Learning Forward. (2012). *Standards into practice: School-based roles. Innovation configuration maps for standards for professional learning.* Oxford, OH: Author.

Learning Forward. (2013). *Standards into practice: School system roles. Innovation configuration maps for standards for professional learning.* Oxford, OH: Author.

Lieberman, A., Miller, L., Roy, P., Hord, S. M., von Frank, V. (2014). *Reach the highest standard in professional learning: Learning communities.* Thousand Oaks, CA: Corwin & Learning Forward.

Marzano, R. J., & Waters, T. (2009). *District leadership that works: Striking the balance.* Bloomington, IN: Solution Tree Press & McREL.

Tschannen-Moran, M. (2004). *Trust matters: Leadership for successful schools.* San Francisco, CA: Jossey-Bass.

Chapter Three

The Case Study

Valerie von Frank

solid evidence that student outcomes are improving, because student achievement is the ultimate goal of professional learning. Professional learning does not take place for its own sake but to enable teachers to teach effectively so that every student achieves.

Often these days it seems we are tempted to focus on our differences rather than seeking the good we can find in the model before us. Reading a case study should invite not only a certain amount of critique but also recognition, if not admiration. Rather than losing the point by focusing on differences and perceived shortcomings, I invite you to consider the standard at hand. Review its main components. Ask how this district exemplifies those elements. Listen carefully to what those at each level of the system said about learning from their vantage point.

Ask probing questions, either as a reader or with colleagues, and use the case as it is meant—for thoughtful discussion of a district's strengths, areas for improvement, and rather than as a comparison with your own or an ideal, as a launching point for discussing how the standard for professional learning strengthens educators' core work and makes possible greater student achievement. When you have delved deeply into the standard itself, the next step is to look within your own district to determine how the standard can be used to improve your system.

At the end of the case study, you will find a set of discussion questions to prime your reflection, analysis, and discussion. We encourage you to meet and discuss this district's leadership with a few colleagues and share your insights with other school and district staff.

How do you change students' lives? Make sure they learn.

When Lexington Public Schools hired superintendent Paul Ash in 2005, he was the fifth leader in seven years, and he faced myriad challenges: High turnover among the leadership team. A budget deficit in the face of a coming recession. Two elementary schools that desperately needed to be renovated. A pending lawsuit over materials teachers used that referenced same-sex couples.

That might have been enough for many leaders to address. But as Ash dug into his new district, he immediately made another important, startling discovery. Not every student in the top-flight district was doing well. About 250 students bused in from Boston under a 1960s voluntary integration program were not among those headed to Harvard. More than half were, instead, routed into special education programs, sometimes in the earliest elementary grades.

For the children who grow up along the winding streets in this well-treed, wealthy, extremely tidy Boston suburb, achievement is expected and accomplishment is the norm. The district as a whole regularly places among the top few in the state for achievement test scores and is recognized as one of the best in the nation (see box, p. 67).

For Ash, though, that wasn't enough. He defined the Lexington district's leadership in terms of a moral code that requires that every child is viewed as having potential to achieve, that *all* children have access to high-quality learning, and that teachers create an environment that supports this level of learning.

For teachers in any extremely high-performing district, where faculty autonomy is as cherished as it often is unchallenged, that isn't a small order. Ash was asking that teachers change how they teach. He believed changes that benefited some students would prove beneficial for all. But teachers would have to develop a different mindset, open their doors and collaborate, and subject their practices to peer scrutiny.

THE LaMURA REPORT CATALYZES CHANGE

Ash's first step to get teachers on board with change was to give staff members information that would convince them of the need. So he asked the just-retired head of the teachers association to study the issue of the achievement gap and report back.

Vito LaMura's report in January 2008 was a turning point. The report clearly documented the extent of the gap in student achievement among racial subgroups; included conversations with parents, students, and staff about why they believed the gaps existed and persisted; outlined research on practices to close the gap; and recommended changes.

The study illustrated gaps between African American and Hispanic students and their White and Asian peers using Massachusetts Comprehensive Assessment System (MCAS) results, and it particularly highlighted the percentage difference in proficiency by grade between White and African American children—a difference that in some instances approached 50 percent or more. The greatest difference, for example, was in fourth-grade math, where 77 percent of

African American children were below proficiency in 2007, compared with 23 percent of Whites, 10 percent of Asians, and 47 percent of Hispanics. Over five years, the gap in math between Whites and African Americans at that grade level had varied between 38 percent and 57 percent.

LEXINGTON PUBLIC SCHOOLS DEMOGRAPHICS

Lexington Public Schools includes one pre-K school, six K–5 buildings, two middle schools, and one high school. The district enrolls 6,785 students, of whom 4.4 percent are African American, 33.2 percent are Asian, 3.4 percent are Hispanic, 0.1 percent are Native American, 53.5 percent are White, and 5.5 percent are multiracial. Of those students, 4 percent are part of the Metropolitan Council for Educational Opportunities (METCO) program in which children are bused from Boston to the Lexington schools. Students eligible for free and reduced-price lunch constitute 8 percent of the student population, and 13.6 percent of students are identified as students with disabilities.

LaMura's report also considered district math assessments in first and second grade, showing that while eight in 10 non-METCO students were in the highest tier, only one in three METCO students were. The gap in reading was smaller, but results indicated a need for special interventions.

The report laid out student grade point averages, secondary school course selections, and special education numbers. METCO children were more likely to be found in special education classes beginning in the early grades, less likely to be found in Advanced Placement and other advanced high school courses, and more likely to have low grade point averages (LaMura, 2008).

LaMura's (2008) report put a local face on the intractable nature of the gap in the nation, state, and district. But more importantly, the report went on to outline a set of core beliefs and assumptions (p. 5):

- Eliminating the achievement gap is not only the right thing to do, but it is essential, given the core purposes of the Lexington Public Schools: (1) academic excellence, (2) respectful and caring relationships, and (3) a culture of reflection, conversation, collaboration, and commitment to continuous improvement.

- The METCO program was long ago woven into the fabric of the Lexington Public Schools, and it continues to contribute mightily and positively to our diversity. It is a program to be cherished and supported to the fullest extent possible.
- Academic ability is a developed (and developable) ability, one that is not simply a function of biological endowment or a fixed aptitude.
- Understanding the fact that academic ability is malleable, we will close the gaps in academic achievement among different groups of students when we have effectively taught all of our students how to learn by using high-quality teaching and instruction in rigorous, relevant curriculum in every classroom.
- Strong, trusting, and encouraging teacher-student relationships will contribute to improving achievement for all students but even more so for African American and Hispanic students, who may have internalized the insidious societal message that low achievement indicates low ability.
- While recognizing the crucial role that parents, community, and culture play in educating all students, the primary focus of our schools must be on what we can control and actually do.
- Schools that concentrate on how their practices affect all students will be more productive and successful than those that blame students, families, poverty, cultural differences, or race for underachievement. Schools can and must have a powerful, positive impact on the achievement of all students.
- We must all continually examine our beliefs and change our practices to counteract the contemporary and historic impacts of racism and discrimination.
- To improve student achievement for all students and thereby close the achievement gap, we must identify and change those aspects of our school culture that impede our gap-closing work.
- With African American and Hispanic children achieving at significantly lower levels than their White and Asian peers, we cannot choose to be color-blind. Emphasizing race in educational discussions and activities may seem controversial or counterintuitive, but it is far more effective than the alternative if our goal is closing the achievement gap.

Ultimately, the report gave credibility to the idea that changes could be made that would affect student achievement.

"It's really opened teachers' eyes to things that weren't working," Whitney Hagins, chair of Lexington High School's science department, told a reporter in 2010 (Sawchuk, 2010).

"Some people said, 'It's not the way I teach; it's a socioeconomic factor'" that leads to student underachievement, said Bill Cole, a Lexington High School social studies teacher and longtime district employee with perspective both as teacher and administrator, in a recent interview. "We had to come to grips with the achievement gap and the results of our actions—or lack of actions. We had to confront our responsibility for the achievement gap."

Ash shared the report publicly with employees and the community. Leaders then made good on each of the report's 16 recommendations. In response to the report's leading recommendation, Ash formed an academic achievement gap committee comprising administrators, faculty, and parents to study ways to better meet all students' needs. (The committee later was renamed the Equity and Excellence Task Force.) The superintendent believed that the changes in how teachers worked with students to raise achievement among some groups of students ultimately would improve learning for all.

He also made clear the direction he wanted the district to head. In an opening speech to staff in August 2008, the superintendent clearly outlined for his audience a moral purpose, that the district needed to "nurture, support, and educate each and every student in our (school) community regardless of race, wealth, background, or special needs" (Devaux et al., 2009).

Ash expressed a clear expectation to all in the district that became almost a mantra: All students get what they need when they need it.

TAKING A STRONG STANCE

In another example of moral fortitude, Ash stewarded the district's stance on a lawsuit filed by two sets of parents citing parental rights. The parents were upset about a couple of books included for kindergarten and early elementary school children. In one instance, a teacher read the class the story of a prince who falls in love with another prince. In another instance, students received a "diversity book bag" with a picture

(Continued)

(Continued)

book that included single-parent families, an extended family, interracial families, animal families, a family without children, and—to the concern of the parents—a family with two dads and a family with two moms. The book concludes by answering the question "Who's in a family?" with "The people who love you the most!"

The parents asked that they receive notice and have the option of excluding their children from exposure to materials or discussions of sexual orientation, same-sex union, or homosexuality (*Parker v. Hurley*, 2006). Same-sex marriage was legalized in Massachusetts in 2004.

When Ash took over as superintendent in 2005–2006, he issued a public statement saying the district would *not* notify parents in advance of "discussions, activities, or materials that simply reference same-gender parents or that otherwise recognize the existence of differences in sexual orientation."

"The issue we were fighting over was a matter of civil rights, and there could be no compromise," Ash later explained (Forg & Foutter, 2015). "Lexington is committed to teaching children about the world they live in, and in Massachusetts, same-sex marriage is legal."

The U.S. District Court for the District of Massachusetts dismissed the suit in February 2007, writing that the parents had voluntarily chosen to send their children to the public schools. "The Constitution does not permit them to prescribe what those children will be taught."

CHANGING CLASSROOM PRACTICE REQUIRES CHANGING THE WORKING CULTURE

Rather than teachers viewing teaching as their purpose, Ash wanted them to see student learning as the necessary outcome. Teachers were asked to reconsider their instructional practices, particularly assessments. Teachers had to focus on determining whether their assessments had been effective; they had to find new ways of reaching students who were not succeeding and at the same time extend lessons for those who demonstrated high achievement. They had to move from using data only from the state standardized exam, which created delays in being able to review and use the results, to a system of regular formative assessments.

"We needed to be clearer about what we wanted students to know and be able to do," said Carol Pilarski, assistant superintendent for curriculum, instruction, and professional learning. "And all had to mean *all*."

Leaders introduced Carol Dweck's concept of a growth mindset and brought in nationally known education experts including Doug Reeves, Richard DuFour, Robert Marzano, Larry Ainsworth, and Grant Wiggins.

"We really needed to transform the culture, to inspire people to do things they hadn't done before," Ash said in an interview. "When we talked to them, we'd say, 'How is this going to come together? What is the data? How are we going to work with these kids who are not learning?'"

Another change involved the staff of the METCO program, who were mostly social workers and counselors. The METCO staff had focused on providing students emotional support rather than on their academic progress, which was left to the teaching staff at Lexington. METCO staff didn't participate in the schools' professional development opportunities. Ash appointed a new leader for the program and changed her title to "academic director," signaling an all-hands-on-deck emphasis on learning. METCO staff began to monitor achievement and advocate more directly for students in the program.

Cole described the changes as "profound."

"There was a hunger on the part of many faculty" for change, Cole said. "We realized we needed it." Still, he acknowledged that the feeling was not universal.

"There was also the feeling, 'Why do I need to change? The kids are doing great.' Well, we had a lot who were succeeding, but there was a range of kids."

LEXINGTON PUBLIC SCHOOLS LEADS THE PACK

- Lexington rates among the top handful of districts in the state for student scores on the state standardized exam.
- The *Boston Globe* and *Boston Magazine* routinely rank the school system as one of the best in Massachusetts.
- In 2014, *Boston Business Journal* ranked the district first in the state.

(Continued)

(Continued)

- The district's professional development was featured in *Education Week*'s November 10, 2010, issue.
- Lexington Public Schools was recognized by ING and the Massachusetts Association of School Business Officials for innovation in reducing costs and effective budget management.
- The *Boston Globe* recognized the district in 2014 as one of the state's best places to work.
- The U.S. Department of Education named Bridge Elementary School a Blue Ribbon School in 2010 and the Clarke Middle School a Blue Ribbon School in 2012.
- *Newsweek* ranked Lexington High School the #1 high school in the state in 2014.
- Lexington High School ranked fourth in the state for SAT scores, with an average score of 1,867.
- Lexington High School is a top feeder school for Harvard University, where one of every 20 students comes from just seven schools each year (Bernhard, 2013).

PROFESSIONAL LEARNING IS PUSHED TO THE FOREFRONT

Ash immediately recognized the need for professional development, said Phyllis Neufeld, head of the Lexington Education Association from 2007 to 2015. He understood the link between educator learning and student learning.

"The environment you need to tackle any big problem is one of continual learning," Ash said. "Professional learning had to be the thread that was consistent in our district goals and school improvement plans. Professional learning would ensure the continuity and coherence of the changes we were trying to make."

So he set to work creating professional development that was "broader in scope, intentional, ongoing and systemic" from a more cafeteria-style approach (Hennessy, 2009). District leadership first worked with the teachers' union to create a professional development committee including teachers and administrators from each school, the assistant superintendent for curriculum, instruction and professional learning, and the coordinator of professional learning.

The committee spent five days in August and September 2009 reviewing research and discussing the issues. Members then developed a statement of purpose, a set of key principles (see box), and drafted professional development standards with strands and indicators to guide design and implementation.

LEXINGTON'S PROFESSIONAL DEVELOPMENT COMMITTEE

Statement of Purpose

Lexington Public Schools is committed to providing a high quality, continuous, and sustained professional development program to all its teachers and other educational professionals. The professional development plan for Lexington Public Schools describes a vision for adult learning that is collaborative, continuous, embedded in daily practice, and focused on student achievement. This model builds on the wealth of knowledge and experience that teachers and practitioners have and expands upon that knowledge and skills. It builds on and strengthens the successes already evident in the district by providing a framework that affords every educator an opportunity to enrich his or her practice. The vision of Lexington Professional Development ensures that standards-based professional development results in continuous professional growth and enhances ongoing student learning.

Key principles

Professional development is most effective when it

- Fosters a culture of continuous improvement
- Improves the learning of all students
- Is research based
- Is data driven
- Is job-embedded
- Supports refinement of practice
- Encourages the use of new strategies
- Promotes shared leadership and responsibility
- Occurs in professional learning communities
- Involves and reflects the diverse nature of the community
- Is adequately supported

Source: Lexington Public Schools, December 16, 2009

The committee elicited feedback through a needs assessment staff questionnaire about what teachers viewed as areas in which they needed to bolster their skills. The committee met for half days twice a month during the workday to look at the data and develop a plan for districtwide learning, along with a timeline.

District leaders had to simultaneously focus on improvements to curriculum, instruction, assessment, and leadership, along with finding the necessary resources to support change in the midst of challenging economic times. The committee was working in the midst of the Great Recession, and Ash decided to use stimulus funds to support professional development, investing in capacity building that would achieve long-term results. He worked with the Lexington Education Foundation (LEF) to understand how critical professional learning is for student achievement and asked for support through faculty grants for professional development and tuition reimbursements.

For example, the foundation provided $24,500 to train all elementary school teachers in administering and evaluating formative assessments and $27,000 for districtwide summer curriculum and instructional development workshops. In addition, the LEF funded a secondary school grant that provided training in professional learning communities.

"We had to build the philosophical mindset where people embrace and engage in continual learning," Pilarski said.

CHANGING STUDENT PERFORMANCE
REQUIRED CHANGING CLASSROOM PRACTICE

Leaders worked to foster more collaborative teacher learning, to create a "learning system," rather than distinct schools or individuals that improved outcomes. They went back to the drawing board to do so.

Curriculum Review

In 2006–2007, the district began a series of curriculum reviews after a decade without systemic evaluation. Teachers' latitude in the classroom meant little coordination was occurring across the grade levels or from grade to grade. Content varied from school to school and even among classrooms at the same grade level in the same school (Ferguson, Ballantine, Bradshaw, & Krontiris, 2015, p. 33).

So teachers spent time in more than 100 summer sessions and in voluntary, unpaid groups after school revamping targeted curricular areas. District leaders also then created districtwide department heads to oversee each curriculum and to coordinate content among the schools.

Ash used an administrative vacancy to restructure the leadership team, adding a position focused on planning, data analysis, and assessment. The district's director of planning and assessment is primarily responsible for analyzing state exam data to identify districtwide needs and consider the need for additional curricular changes. Ash committed to transparency from the start, making data public and acknowledging areas that needed improvement to all within the district and community.

Professional Learning Communities

In the first year of his leadership, Ash had asked teachers to work together on yearlong action research projects to identify possible problem areas and potential solutions. Teachers were asked to share their results publicly for the first time.

Then, after a year of teacher collaboration on action research, Ash asked all staff in 2006–2007 to participate in professional learning communities (PLCs) to strategize ways to improve their teaching for all students.

Ash brought in nationally recognized PLC speakers Richard and Rebecca DuFour to introduce the concept, which centers on educators' commitment to work together to address core questions:

1. What do we want each student to learn?

2. How will we know each student has learned it?

3. How will we respond when a student experiences difficulty in learning?

4. How will we respond when a student already knows it?

Teachers worked in grade-level or subject groups to set learning benchmarks, examined student data, planned lessons, and discussed instructional strategies. They had to begin to think of peers as collaborators, rather than only colleagues.

Leonard Swanton, coordinator of professional learning and special projects, said the focus began to shift to deeper, sustained analysis of student learning across a grade level or within a content area. Groups that had worked together to plan field trips had to shift their focus to center on analyzing student work. For some educators, the change was challenging. Solving problems collaboratively meant public discussion of student performance. Teachers whose students were achieving at standard needed to understand why they needed to collaborate, and teachers with pockets of low-performing students had to trust their colleagues as group members began to share input and ideas.

"We moved from the idea of teaching in separate silos to gathering information as a team on student learning and searching for instructional entry points for students who were not making expected progress," Swanton said. "There was a shift from delivering curriculum to being deliberate and thoughtful in figuring out what students had learned from that curriculum delivery. There was increased collaboration in examining the impact of targeted instruction so that there would be improved learning for *all* students."

Neufeld, the head of the teachers' association, said the emphasis on PLCs is on learning strategies that teachers can use in the classroom the next day. Teams began to shift from the "one-off" questions about student work that they had focused on in action research to questions that would have broader impact on practices. For example, when four fifth-grade teachers discovered they all were struggling with a particular strand of the curriculum, they worked together to develop a variation on a Japanese lesson study to help one another address the challenge.

Teachers created learning objectives for their meetings. They were held accountable for outcomes; they posted agendas and kept minutes of their meetings to share with their department heads.

The district ensured time in the workday for learning communities. Teachers were given a minimum of one planning period each week to collaborate in grade-level or content teams. The protected time is now written into the teaching contract.

"It's rare now to see teachers working at their desks independently," Swanton said. "Most of the time, you see them consulting with colleagues."

"Teachers are willing to be present for each other," Lexington High School Principal Laura Lasa said. "They've gotten over the fear and wanting to be perfect."

Some school leaders supplement PLC time with professional development during regular faculty meeting times after school. Principals have learned rather than covering a list of administrative agenda items to embrace learning as an agent for change. While topics are connected to districtwide goals, leaders can be responsive to specific school targets. For example, some schools identified a need to address changes in their student populations and brought in experts on the Caribbean experience of traditional learning or the cultural norms of the Indian peninsula to help teachers understand these students' lens for learning.

Changes in Assessment

The district set as a goal having the elementary and middle schools adopt common formative assessments by 2010, followed a year later by the high school, and provided professional development for teachers on designing effective formative assessments.

Teachers worked together in their PLCs and in data teams to develop common benchmarks and to design pre- and posttests for subject areas, tying them to the revised curriculum. In the lower grades, the assessments tied directly to new standards-based report cards.

At the high school, the changes went beyond coordination to a new understanding of ways to tie assessments directly to improved instruction. Lasa said that high school teachers were asked to examine their grading practices along with their lessons. They were asked to more precisely evaluate the balance of students' academic habits, understanding of the material, and skill development.

She said teachers began to consider whether assessments were leaving students behind. "A lot of times, grades reflect compliance behavior, such as turning in homework. Maybe it's not an achievement gap but more about the child's experience in the classroom."

For example, when one student raised the question with a teacher about why the only assessment was writing a paper, the teacher decided to provide alternatives, such as the option of doing a project, for students to demonstrate their learning.

Lasa said few teachers rely on Scantron exams now. Instead, students are asked to demonstrate understanding in more depth by writing essays and providing evidence to support thesis statements. In math, students are required to show their work rather than just bubbling in an answer on a multiple-choice test. Because teachers ask students to demonstrate their thinking in multiple ways, teachers have a better sense of students' understanding. In addition, they have added "mini-assessments" throughout their courses to rely less on end-of-course summary assessments. They are able then to use the results of formative assessments to adjust their teaching during the term.

Data Teams

In addition to learning communities examining student data to identify struggling students, teachers also are part of data teams that review information to identify trends along with specific student performance and teams may make recommendations for teacher interventions. Data teams comprising teachers, counselors, and administrators meet every six weeks to review collective and individual student data for every school.

"We are finding the sweet spot of using data to inform our instruction in deep and effective ways," Swanton said.

The district developed a tiered response targeting students not learning at the pace needed to meet the benchmarks. Now teachers more actively refer students for interventions. Secondary school students are held accountable for taking a study hall rather than physical education or an elective if they need more help.

"We had to have unwavering conversations about providing academic support in school, during the day, for students who were not performing," Lasa said.

Coaching

Next, leaders added coaching and other site-based professional learning into the changes. English language learning specialists work with students while also helping teachers develop their skills to support this special population.

The district has math and literacy coaches at the elementary level who work with teachers in the classroom. Rather than having specialists who worked directly with students, leaders converted more than a dozen such positions to coaches who help model instruction in the classroom and work with grade-level teachers on lesson planning. Ash also reallocated funds to add math coaches.

Leaders revamped teacher schedules to offer time for coaching and peer observation. Teachers began to open themselves up to their peers.

"Coaching became contagious," Pilarski said. "When teachers saw the effect it could have on teaching and learning, they wanted it."

ADDITIONAL INSTRUCTION FOR STUDENTS

District leaders also increased student instructional time for those who need it.

To focus on closing gaps from the start, the school system added full-day kindergarten and began interventions early for math and language. Across the district, teachers learned not only about differentiating instruction but also about responding when students were behind, as early as that first year in kindergarten.

At the elementary level, data teams identified students who might benefit from math or literacy instruction, and those children worked with specialists in one- or two-hour blocks respectively each day.

All METCO middle school students, not just those who were struggling, were offered an extra hour of instruction each day. The bus to Boston took students home an hour later, leaving time for the commuters to participate in after-school activities such as tutoring. Teachers were paid a small stipend to help students with homework and bolster their skills. The district created a three-week middle school summer math camp for sixth- and seventh-grade METCO students, a chance to strengthen their understanding before high school.

Just before entering high school, METCO students could attend a summer school to get to know teachers and other high school students. Then, during the year, they could drop in during the day for peer tutoring sessions.

The high school also offered a homework club twice a week and a learning center for academic support, with 75 peer tutors offering support to those falling behind. METCO students were offered "extended learning" after school at the high school level in math and English language. Students who participated in the METCO program could take advantage of hour-long tutoring sessions led by teachers and specialists on 20 Thursdays during the year after school.

High-performing African American and Latino students in tenth grade or above could participate in a scholars' program that offered mentoring in small groups, with four or five students receiving support from a faculty member in weekly sessions.

THE RESULT IS IMPROVEMENT

The convergence of professional learning and special attention to specific student populations helped boost student achievement even as teachers saw that they *could* make a difference for all students.

Ash asked to be included in a special Harvard University's Graduate School of Education study authored by a team led by Ron Ferguson, whose focus is on educational inequities, to verify the improvements. Ferguson's team found that in Lexington, "both excellence and equity have been increasing" (Ferguson et al., 2015, p. 29).

"We find that Lexington has effectively raised achievement among African American students as well as in the district overall," the report states (Ferguson et al., 2015, p. 2), as "low-performing students from every background benefit from the deep dive of the data teams and RTI, and every single student benefits from a curriculum aligned around common standards and teachers who collaborate to better their instructional practice" (Ferguson et al., 2015, p. 33).

In fact, by the end of the 2013–2014 school year, every African American tenth grader was rated proficient or advanced on the English Language Arts (ELA) section of the state standardized assessment, and 96 percent were proficient or advanced in math, equating to just a couple of students missing the mark.

- Grade 10 African American ELA MCAS scores increased from 43 percent proficient and advanced in 2007 to 100 percent in 2014.
- Grade 10 African American mathematics scores increased from 68 percent proficient and advanced in 2007 to 96 percent in 2014.
- Between 2006 and 2014, SAT scores rose 294 points for African American students, from 1,237 to 1,531 on the reading, math, and writing portions.

Ash believed that raising achievement for African Americans would raise achievement for all students. That has proven true.

Grade 10 ELA special education MCAS scores increased from 79 percent proficient and advanced in 2010 to 100 percent in 2014; and Grade 10 special education students' mathematics scores increased from 81 percent proficient and advanced in 2010 to 95 percent in 2014.

"Districtwide instructional changes have cultivated deep collaboration between teachers; targeted interventions through the effective use of student data; and built a home-grown, but exceptionally deep professional learning program," Ferguson's report concludes.

BACKLASH AND REINVESTMENT

Moving teachers out of their silos was not without some resistance. Teaching and professional learning changed dramatically in just a few years, and experienced, smart teachers were frustrated at what some perceived as an assault on their autonomy and perhaps professionalism. Spending planning time working with colleagues was stressful. Some saw Ash's relatively quick changes as "top-down," made without enough faculty input.

Leaders were not surprised that change resulted in significant pushback. Pilarski said that in hindsight, administrators might have been more purposeful in helping teachers understand the benefits of the action research, learning teams, and the value of the work to long-term student achievement goals. The leaders acknowledge that the links between various efforts may not always have been made clear to staff implementing them.

"Five years ago, there appeared to many to be separate initiatives that did not seem connected," Pilarski said. Multiple committees with sometimes competing priorities made different recommendations, from the Excellence and Equity Committee's summary (Lexington Public Schools, 2009) and the state's Coordinated Program Review to the New England Association of Secondary Schools and Colleges' accreditation report. Professional learning communities' work seemed early on to be unrelated to school or district goals. Some teachers left the district. Morale was low.

Ash responded with characteristic transparency and commitment to using the issue as a learning opportunity. The superintendent hired a consultant to work with an internal committee on a climate study. Consultant Bruce Wellman's study found that

"Lexington's drive to close the achievement gap between special education, English language learners, minority students and traditionally successful populations has come at a cost to staff relations" (Wellman, 2012).

Rather than keeping the results quiet, Ash then aired the grievances publicly as district leaders sought ways to respond. He created a climate wellness committee to survey staff each year and report to school committee members. At the same time, he remained on message with the commitment to all students learning and made sure that the district operating budget supported continued professional learning to accomplish the goal.

The commitments sent a clear message about the district's values. And momentum shifted.

"We needed to have a background of trust," Ash said later in an interview, "of people who want to learn more. We wanted a system in which anyone in the district can be a leader and take on a new challenge, a place where people *want* to collaborate."

That distributed leadership approach was in evidence in November 2014 when Lexington had a districtwide peer share day, titled "Lexington Learns." Teachers who had become experts in different areas, such as brain development, led sessions for their peers on 130 high-quality, vetted topics in their specialties during a full day of professional learning.

"It was like a little university," Ash said. Nearly 800 teachers participated, with about 170 teachers and administrators leading sessions.

Teachers who had never stood up in front of one another shared their knowledge—and learned from peers. The mutual respect and relational trust needed as the foundation of a learning system was firmly in place, and teachers were more interested and excited to be learning from their colleagues.

As Ash noted, "In a system with low trust, you're not developing leaders or the capacity of people. Then you end up with a series of initiatives. You're going to get some progress, but it will not be widespread or sustainable."

Pilarski said staff have undergone a profound shift. "We created a growth mindset among the staff, developed a collaborative spirit, and distributed leadership," she said. "This allowed us to become an even better and stronger learning community."

LEXINGTON FACES THE FUTURE

"There is a long-running debate among educators and policymakers about whether schools can counteract social inequalities in children's families and neighborhoods," according to Sean Reardon (2015). The Stanford education researcher concludes, however, that neither poverty nor race fully accounts for differences in student achievement, and he says that schools can reduce inequality more effectively than they have in the past.

Lexington Public Schools' success is the evidence for Reardon's assertion that the gap can be overcome—with a unified effort and targeted attention. Professional learning has become a living part of the district's identity and now is just the way things are done.

Teachers are not satisfied just with teaching. They want to know that students are learning, to look at student work, and to analyze data together. Faculty know more about how students learn and what strategies may work better with different children. They also have learned how to learn, so that they can continue to address changing student needs in a changing world.

The district increased its capacity to serve the whole school community, with leaders identifying the need, creating a sense of urgency to meet it, developing an action plan, outlining professional development, focusing on data to enhance instruction for a continual cycle of learning, and supporting professional learning communities. Educators in the system revamped the curriculum and defined and sequenced benchmarks, and teachers worked together to develop common assessments.

"We really created a culture where people are passionately interested in developing the individual capacity of teachers and schools to learn and improve, and the district's capacity at the collective level to be a learning system," Ash said.

Leaders, from administrators to teacher leaders, are leaving a legacy. And while the recorded voice callers hear when they dial into the district's phone system is no longer Ash's since he retired as superintendent in June 2015, Lexington's forward momentum will likely continue.

Ash said the district has new energy: "Lexington is a true learning organization where teachers are interested in and committed to continually improving their practices."

VIEW FROM THREE SEATS

Bill Cole

Lexington High School social studies teacher

It was hard for us 10 years ago to have the conversation about improvement. We have an elite school system in many ways. High-level programs are woven into the curriculum. The feeling among staff was, "Why do I need to change? The kids are doing great." Well, the upper 20 percent to 40 percent of students are ridiculously strong. Many are the children of university faculty members in the Boston area. But we had to make sure to provide for the well-rounded student who works hard and is just developing skills, who is not going to take courses over the summer. We had a lot of kids who were succeeding, but there was a range. And there's always room for professional growth.

Over the last seven or eight years, we've seen a change within the district. An increased amount of training and coursework is available, and the focus has been more on pedagogy and interventions, things beyond looking only at improving content. We have also focused on developing curricular knowledge and revamping the curriculum.

We've had national leaders come to help us. Professional development is always funded, and people can take courses that make them better teachers. The real change was through peer-to-peer, grow-your-own professional learning. In the last few years, it is not just the classroom teachers, either, who are involved. We are bringing the paraprofessionals and aides in to professional development.

Lexington Learns, a one-day session in which teachers provided sessions for colleagues, was a good opportunity for staff to lead and learn. In total, we have five days a year of professional development. We also have classes in the afternoons outside of the school day. And we go to one another's classes to observe. We have learning opportunities in the summer on our own time.

For me, professional development is not a matter of having an impact on my salary. I'm just trying to do my job better. If we're going to be demanding of students, we need to be demanding of ourselves.

Laura Lasa

Lexington High School principal

Lexington is a high-performing district that runs on steroids. We are uber everything. The high school, with 2,200 students, functions more like a liberal arts college. That's the way our culture has always been because there is a commitment to and belief in high-quality education for all students. It's a reflection of the community's expectations.

We were already doing a tremendous amount of professional learning. In the last five to six years, we've branched out, though, to focus on pedagogy, strategy, brain-based learning, social-emotional issues. We're trying to feed all those aspects into content area knowledge. We had to come to terms with the urgency of meeting the needs of about 15 percent of the population that was not achieving.

We began to work with coteaching, collaborating on instruction. We needed to make the curriculum more engaging. We needed to provide resources and support to students who were not meeting the standards without slowing the curriculum down.

At first, it was not easy for everyone to open up their practices. The initial reaction was, "What's broken?" Some teachers took it personally that they were being asked to change their approach to instruction in particular courses or with particular populations of students. Now they understand it has to do with continuing to get better, and it's every teacher's responsibility to reach all students in the classroom and through schoolwide supports. We need to be willing to reinvent the way we do things.

The commitment to professional learning is not something teachers just talk about. Educators put in a lot of additional time outside the workday to improve their instruction. Teachers have asked for peer observation, and they work closely with colleagues in their departments to align curriculum and develop new strategies.

If we're organized as leaders, we can arrange this kind of peer learning. Lexington teachers are very self-reflective and self-critical. Our push is continuing to help them balance their reflections with feedback in order to put them into action. That's just the fabric of our district now. It's where we're going in the service of all students.

Carol Pilarski

Assistant superintendent for curriculum, instruction, and professional development

Learning for *all* students was this goal, but it was never clearly articulated. When we articulated it—that *all* has to mean *all*, not just those who already could be performing at a high level—we changed.

(Continued)

(Continued)

We said that success has to mean the population of METCO students, special education students, and the increasing number of English language learners. And despite Lexington's being considered affluent, we do have a population of low-income students and an increased number of homeless students. These seemed to be the populations we were not serving as well as the 80 percent to 85 percent who were doing extremely well. So we began to focus on that percentage that was not achieving as highly. Our experience was that with this effort, the tide raises all boats. All students were benefitting.

PLCs began concurrently. People were collegial and were accustomed to working together, but collaborating moved teachers toward greater understanding of how to be more effective with all students. Teachers had been closing their doors and doing well independently, but they had not realized how to work more efficiently, the benefits of mutual ownership and responsibility, and not just for student performance but for each other's success in supporting student achievement.

Professional learning is not only attending conferences. It's reading, research, and sharing information. As administrators, we don't want to be the gurus of professional learning. We want teachers to learn from teachers. Building a culture of continual learning with ownership and responsibility helped us grow as a district.

Developing professional learning is a journey of ups and downs. It requires persistence and patience. I would advise other districts that an important shift in culture does not happen because you wish it. To reach convergence and consensus among staff so that they are collectively and collaboratively moving together requires continual tweaking. It takes consistent focus on student learning and a consistent focus on the message. It is never over.

APPLYING THE CASE

REINTERPRETING THE LEXINGTON CASE FOR DIFFERENT SETTINGS

Karen Seashore Louis | Shirley M. Hord

Positioning the Case: Generalizing Lessons for Action

As you read the Lexington case, did you wonder what it says for you? Perhaps your district and high school is smaller or less affluent.

Alternatively, maybe you are in a multi–high school urban setting and wonder how to achieve some of these results. Maybe you are not the superintendent and wonder how you can get started as a "leader in the middle."

Here are a few suggestions, based on our combined 80 decades of working with schools that face similar problems:

- Find a problem that requires action by multiple parties, both inside and outside the school. In Lexington's case, it was the achievement gap, but each community's sense of priorities is different.

  o One rural district that we worked with suffered from "out-migration" and an aging population. The problem that brought teachers, parents, and the community together was how to serve the needs of an increasing Hispanic population in ways that could stabilize the school population and community.

- The big story of the Lexington case is engagement of multiple constituencies before any significant reallocation of resources occurs.

  o Paul Ash, the superintendent, reached out first to the teachers' union and then to a group of local leaders who helped to raise money and support for the schools. Your district may not have a community and parent-based foundation, but that need not deter you from mobilizing support.

- Generate discussions that ensure that all (or most) major constituencies see the problem as focused on students but best addressed by adult learning.

  o Ash engaged administrators and teachers in addressing basic questions around shared values and practices well before more practical, data-driven analysis. The sharing of discussions across schools and within communities that may have seen themselves as "our school" and "our students" to find a shared focus created a systemwide commitment.

- Bring in an outside facilitator who can help with the process of engagement.

  o Lexington was able to pay national consultants at various stages. Many districts cannot do this. But we have ample evidence that effective superintendents (and other school leaders) know where the sources of local and free (or less expensive) expertise can be found. In many states, this may be a regional educational service center or a local university, but there are usually other local/regional resources.

- Specialized coaches are nice, but not always necessary—effective PLCs and peer observation can provide the same support.

  o Coaching is one of the more popular staffing innovations in larger districts. However, we have worked in many smaller districts and individual schools where teachers use alternative ways to open up their classrooms and foster effective reflection.

  o One inner-city school that we worked with recently hired a local consultant to train teachers to do classroom observations—the goal was not to provide the observed teacher with feedback but to allow the teacher who was observing to reflect on his or her own practice. Such structured observations allowed new conversations about teaching and learning (including equity) to emerge within a year—more effectively than the subject coaches that were provided by the district.

  o Another district, more similar to Lexington but less affluent, provided coaching training to a larger number of teachers, who could then act as peer observers.

- Anticipate the normal crises that come with any significant change in practice—and be prepared to pause, reflect, and adjust.

  o The "implementation dip" has been part of the vocabulary of change for 30 years. Lexington used an external consultant to address the issue, but many districts and schools that we have worked with get similar results by acknowledging discomfort, allowing it to be freely expressed, and using "positive engagement" to regain trust.

  o Again, Lexington had the capacity to hire an external consultant to do this work, and most large districts will need expert help, but the underlying principles of appreciative inquiry and participatory diagnosis do not require this in smaller settings.

Additional Discussion Questions

1. Consider the five fundamental tasks of leadership for professional learning (Chapter 1). How are these tasks reflected in the case? How would you address each of these in your context?

2. Consider the six research-based strategies deemed necessary for implementing new practices (Chapter 2). Are any of these strategies evident in the case? If so, select one and share a mental image of this occurrence that you see in your thoughts.

3. How did the superintendent in the case initiate his plans for the district's new way of conducting its business of making certain that every student is a successful learner? In your judgment, what actions were taken, and how could you apply these actions in your district?

4. Compare and contrast the model of leadership reflected by the superintendent in the case with the research-informed leadership model shared in Chapter 1. Which factors from the Chapter 1 model may be found in the superintendent's leadership? What benefits, if any, were contributed by these factors to the case's story, and so what?

5. Who else in the case was given (or took on) leadership responsibilities? Which leadership tasks (Chapter 1) or implementation strategies (Chapter 2) were delegated or shared? How might that work in your setting?

6. Ponder the array of ideas, concepts, or constructs presented in Chapter 1. Select an idea that caught your attention, review it, and explain why it caught your attention, impacting you either positively or negatively. If the effect was negative, how might you tweak it to put a positive spin on it?

References

Bernhard, M. P. (2013, December 13). The making of a Harvard feeder school. *The Harvard Crimson.* Available at http://www.thecrimson.com/article/2013/12/13/making-harvard-feeder-schools

Devaux, P., DeVito, F., Hearns, J. L., McAuliffe, J. (2009, October). *Lexington Public Schools review of district systems and practices addressing the differentiated needs of all students.* Malden, MA: Massachusetts Department of Elementary and Secondary Education.

Ferguson, R., Ballantine, A., Bradshaw, R., Krontiris, C. (2015, June). *Narrowing achievement gaps in Lexington Public Schools.* Lexington, MA: Lexington Public Schools.

Forg, L., & Foutter, M. (2015). *Dr. Paul Ash.* Retrieved from http://84946556.nhd.weebly.com

Hennessy, J. M. (2009). *Update on year one of the professional development committee.* Lexington Public Schools internal document.

LaMura, V. A. (2008, January). *The achievement gap in the Lexington Public Schools: Documentation, research, and recommendations.* Lexington, MA: Lexington Public Schools.

Lexington Public Schools. (2009, May 5). *Action plan for equity and excellence.* Achievement Gap Task Force.

Lexington Public Schools. (2009, December 16). *Professional development overview.* Professional Development Committee.

Parker v. Hurley, 514 F. 3d 87 (1st Cir. 2008)

Reardon, S. (2015). *State of the states: The poverty and inequality report.* Palo Alto, CA: Stanford Center on Poverty and Inequality.

Sawchuk, S. (2010, November 10). Mass. district strives for teacher "learning system." *Education Week.*

Wellman, B. (2012). *Report to the Lexington school committee and employees of the Lexington Public Schools improving professional relationships in the Lexington Public Schools.* Lexington Public Schools internal document.

Index

CORWIN

A SAGE Company

The Corwin logo—a raven striding across an open book—represents the union of courage and learning. Corwin is committed to improving education for all learners by publishing books and other professional development resources for those serving the field of PreK–12 education. By providing practical, hands-on materials, Corwin continues to carry out the promise of its motto: **"Helping Educators Do Their Work Better."**

Advancing professional learning for student success

Learning Forward (formerly National Staff Development Council) is an international association of learning educators committed to one purpose in K–12 education: Every educator engages in effective professional learning every day so every student achieves.

Solutions you want. Experts you trust. Results you need.

Author Consulting

Author Consulting

On-site professional learning with sustainable results! Let us help you design a professional learning plan to meet the unique needs of your school or district. www.corwin.com/pd

Institutes

Institutes

Corwin Institutes provide collaborative learning experiences that equip your team with tools and action plans ready for immediate implementation. www.corwin.com/institutes

eCourses

eCourses

Practical, flexible online professional learning designed to let you go at your own pace. www.corwin.com/ecourses

Read2Earn

Read2Earn

Did you know you can earn graduate credit for reading this book? Find out how: www.corwin.com/read2earn

Contact an account manager at (800) 831-6640 or visit **www.corwin.com** for more information.